IN SEARCH OF
COMMON GROUND

IN SEARCH OF
COMMON GROUND

Conversations with *ERIK H. ERIKSON*
and *HUEY P. NEWTON*

Introduced by *KAI T. ERIKSON*

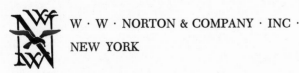
W · W · NORTON & COMPANY · INC ·
NEW YORK

FIRST EDITION

Library of Congress Cataloging in Publication Data
Erikson, Erik Homburger, 1902–
    In search of common ground.
    1. Newton, Huey P.   2. Erikson, Erik Homburger,
1902–   3. Black Panther Party.   I. Newton, Huey P.
II. Title.
E185.615.E74   322.4'2'0924   73–4191

ISBN 0–393–05483–7

1 2 3 4 5 6 7 8 9 0

Contents

IN SEARCH OF
COMMON GROUND

Introduction

By Kai T. Erikson

THE FOLLOWING is a record of conversations which took place on two separate occasions, the first at Yale University in New Haven, Connecticut, in early February 1971, and the second in Oakland, California, about two months later. The most prominent voices in these discussions belong to Huey P. Newton, then known as Supreme Commander of the Black Panther Party (the title has since been dropped), and Erik H. Erikson, Professor Emeritus of Human Development and Lecturer in Psychiatry at Harvard University.

These discussions are almost a study in contrasts. To begin with, the two principals had to reach across a number of differences in outlook and experience to begin their search for common ground. And then, too, the meetings themselves could hardly have been more dissimilar. The New Haven conference was large and structured, and the dialogue which emerged from it was occasionally marked by a certain formality of address and even wariness of approach. The Oakland talks, on the other hand, were a good deal more informal, and the record taken at that time reflects the increased comfort that comes from closer acquaintance and more relaxed surroundings.

So it is hard to know how to introduce this volume. Everyone connected with the meetings is aware that the record contains a number of false starts and missed chances as well as moments of understanding and insight; that the flow of conversation is lively at some points and halting at others. But encounters of this kind do not happen very often and are worth preserving. In preparing this transcript for publication, then, we have taken our title quite seriously: what follows is not meant as a summary of the common ground reached during the talks but as a record of the search itself.

I

"Good" conversation is usually thought to depend upon a common vocabulary, a mutual frame of reference, a shared repertory of symbol and meaning. If this is so, the exchange of views recorded here could barely qualify for that title. The two principals approached their meeting from wholly different worlds of experience: indeed, they were drawn to one another largely for that reason. The first is a thirty-year-old black revolutionary, a man whose perspective on life has been tempered by a childhood on the Oakland streets, years of raw conflict with police, and a long period of study and thought in a California jail. The second is a seventy-year-old European immigrant whose outlooks have been shaped in the gentler climates of German gymnasia, Viennese psychoanalytic institutes, and American clinical and academic settings. Both are soft-spoken men, but the one is intense, urgent, almost muscular in tone, while the other is reflective and reserved, unhurried in speech, as if he is used to conveying some sense of himself through words rather than actions. The younger of the two men is in a hurry. He has recently been released from prison and is aware that he may have to go back soon, and in the meantime he serves as the administrative leader and chief ideologue of a movement, an important symbol to those who follow him and those who fear him, a man very much caught up in the historical currents he has helped set into motion. The older man is in less of a hurry. He has recently retired from active teaching, having reached a certain level of eminence in his chosen work and chosen country, and he is known for a calm and thoughtful kind of scholarship. On the surface, at least, the two men would appear to be worlds apart.

Good conversation is also supposed to take place in "natural" surroundings, and on this score, too, the circumstances would have to be described as somewhat mixed. The first round of talks took place in a handsomely appointed university library, a thing of leather and tapestry and endless shelves of books. Eighteen people sat around a huge mahogany table and an equal number of onlookers formed another circle outside them —behind Newton, a half-ring of comrades and travel companions, and behind Erikson, in awkward symmetry, a half-ring of Yale people. Without any conscious intent, the stage had been set for a confrontation. The second round of talks took place in Newton's Oakland apartment. Four people sat around a small breakfast table, drinking coffee in the early hours and moving on to heartier fare as the long days drew to an end. It was a congenial setting in every way—and yet there was a hint of alarm in the air, a sense of urgency, made more real by the security precautions that (in those days, at any rate) enveloped Newton wherever he went.

Good conversation is supposed to depend on some degree of spontaneity, too. People "strike up" conversations or "fall into" them, and the exchange which results is thought to be meaningful to the extent that it develops its own rhythm, its own pace and flow, independent of external pressures. In many respects, the Oakland meetings were to have this quality, but the New Haven meetings required so much coordination and planning, such attention to schedules and agendas, that they began to assume the character of a high-level diplomatic encounter. In the first place, the meetings brought together two busy men with strong feelings of responsibility to the callings they represented

—and each of them, in his own way, knew that he was taking chances. In the second place, the affair attracted a good deal more publicity than we had bargained for or knew how to handle, and this added appreciably to the sense of secrecy and excitement that emerged. In the third place, one basic difference between a simple conversation and a formal conference is that the former has no objective other than a reasonably coherent exchange of views while the latter is organized to produce something—a treaty or an understanding or a document or something else. We were clearly unable to resist the thought that a useful book might issue from the discussions, and this meant that the meeting was conducted in a setting full of tape recorders, microphones, coils of wire, and a general mood of expectancy. Those persons who sat around the table, for all their absorption in one another, never really lost the feeling that they were part of a spectacle.

Good conversation, finally, is supposed to be a relaxed exchange, a product of leisure, located a little outside the binding urgencies of the moment. These conversations, though, took place at a time when the various participants could not step away from the historical currents in which they were immersed, and this had an important influence on the tone of the proceedings. Among those currents the following should be noted:

• that Yale University, the host of the first gathering, had recently recovered from what had been properly described as the most dangerous year in its history—a danger that had been occasioned by a trial of Black Panthers, sharpened by the indignation of Panther spokesmen, and then greatly reduced by the cool good sense of those very same people. Yale had suffered no lasting damage during the emergencies of May Day, but its nerves were raw and its feelings about the Panthers very mixed.

• that Huey Newton came to New Haven as the trial of Bobby Seale and Ericka Huggins was reaching its climax, and left New Haven at the very moment a painful and trying rift was emerging within the ranks of the Black Panther Party. (I do not know much about that occurrence, but it is a matter of public record that Connie Mathews, the Party Secretary, and Michael Tabor, one of the New York 21, abruptly deserted the Party and moved underground just as the meetings in New Haven came to an end.) Newspapers were full of stories about the inner turmoil of the Party in the month that followed, and all of this was capped, just a day or two before we met again in Oakland, by the news that Eldridge Cleaver, too, had broken with Newton from his outpost in Algeria.

• that most of the Yale students and faculty members who participated in the discussions—like academics everywhere—were still trying to come to reasonable terms with the invasion of Cambodia, the shootings at Jackson State and Kent State, the Panther trials, and all the other events of that fateful season. This meant that they were deeply uneasy about their place in the world, vaguely concerned about the privileged positions they held, and anxious to learn how their sharpened sense of responsibility could be converted into a kind of active commitment.

So the historical moment is very much a part of these conversations, even if it was rarely discussed as such. Transcripts, of course, do not record anything but the flat words spoken during an exchange (and those imperfectly), but perhaps one can help convey the insistency and pitch of the conversations by noting that the participants spent a good part of the time reaching across the table, leaning toward one another, as if to create something of a physical communion when words seemed limp and unequal to the task.

The reader should listen to what follows with two ears. The first should be tuned to content—the ideology of revolution, the philosophy of psychoanalysis, the search for convergences. The second ear, meantime, should attend to the tone and temper of the conversations themselves. A number of differences between Huey Newton and Erik Erikson may be registered in the words they speak, but none so clearly as the points of departure from which they pursue their arguments. The ideology is relentless, heavy, reliant upon a closed system of logic—as it must be. The philosophy is contemplative, conscious of self, making a virtue of doubt—as it should be. The ideology seeks certainty and offers it as a basis for conviction; the philosophy relies on uncertainty and views conviction itself as a legitimate topic of study.

All of this is reflected in subtle nuances of tone—the differences in cadence as one speaker gives way to another, the differences in emphasis as points of argument are pursued across the table, and so on.

II

The Yale meetings began with a telephone call in early January of 1971. The call was from Donald Freed, a member of the Panther Defense Committee who was in New Haven to write a book about the Seale-Huggins trial. Freed noted that Newton was planning a visit to New Haven in the immediate future and had expressed some interest in meeting with a group of Yale students during his stay. I was Master of one of Yale's twelve residential colleges and therefore in a position to issue the invitation and make the necessary arrangements. Would I be interested? The answer, of course, was yes: the students of Trumbull College would have the rare good fortune of meeting with and talking to Newton in what we hoped would become a relaxed, informal, intimate seminar without any excitement or publicity.

Now it happens that Erik H. Erikson and I have known one another fairly well for forty years or more, and he is, besides, a Fellow of Trumbull College; so it occurred to us a few days later that he might be interested in becoming a part of the gathering. Both Erikson and Newton agreed, and a date was set.

In the month that followed, however, our simple seminar threatened to escalate into something approaching an international convention. We had decided (as everyone does these days) to make a tape recording of the proceedings, partly because it seemed like a good idea to have a transcript on file and partly because—who knows—the discussions might be worth publishing. As if in response to that vagrant thought, several publishers were soon inquiring about the meetings, and they were followed in close order by journalists, photographers, and even a film producer, all of them wanting to record the event.

None of us knew how to handle so much interest, and by the time the conversations actually began we had moved from the spare informality of Trumbull College to the library of the Yale University Press and had retreated behind a virtual curtain of secrecy. All of this, as we should have known, only sharpened the already strong impression that some kind of clandestine negotiation was in progress, intriguing the press even further and creating new ripples of alarm elsewhere.

Opinions throughout the Yale community varied widely about the desirability of the meetings. A campus which had so recently heard angry threats and smelled tear gas and experienced the unfamiliar sensation of being vulnerable and out of control was understandably apprehensive about the whole thing. A few professors and more than a few alumni expressed misgivings (although no one made a move to interfere), and many townspeople were clearly irritated. The tough and capable Chief of University Police, Louis Cappiello, went directly to work on security arrangements with what turned out to be the wisest remark of the season: "Hell, Kai, what's a university for?"

Yale got its first look at Huey Newton the night before the meetings began. The Panthers had rented Woolsey Hall, a huge marbled auditorium in the center of the campus, to expose Newton to the larger Yale community; and they managed the event in a way the student body would not soon forget. All the entrances to the hall were sealed save one, and each of the fourteen hundred persons who entered was frisked by cordial but very businesslike Panthers and invited to donate a dollar or two to the Party. To students who had passed through those doors many times before—to hear Kingman Brewster deliver a baccalaureate address or hear Artur Rubinstein offer a recital—the effect was disconcerning and maybe even menacing. The Panthers in charge worked with a discipline and measured courtesy that could only be called military, and as the audience filtered slowly through the security screen into the auditorium, they were met by walls full of posters and slogans as well as ranks of unsmiling

Panthers guarding the entrances to the stage and balcony. Once seated, they waited for almost two hours.

Newton finally walked onto the stage around ten o'clock. On such occasions he wears a sharply creased uniform shirt made from black material and carries a baton tipped with what looks like a silver bullet: this was the Huey Newton the audience knew, the Huey Newton who stares out from endless posters with a black beret on his head, a bandolier hung over his shoulder, and an automatic rifle in his hands. Once at the podium, however, a new and unfamiliar Newton introduced himself. He put on steel-rimmed spectacles, laid down his baton, smiled a greeting, and then spoke for two hours in his thin, controlled voice without once using expressions like "pig" or once employing any ornamental rhetoric, drifting instead over such heady terrain as dialectical materialism, the philosophies of Hegel, Kant, Peirce, and Marx, the psychologies of Freud, Jung, James, and Erikson, and a number of other subjects as abstract as anything ever presented in a Yale classroom. Virtually everyone was disappointed, as Newton knew they would be—radicals because they wanted tougher words to stiffen their periodically limping spirits, moderates because they were anticipating another kind of entertainment, and conservatives because the sheer temperateness of Newton's tone deflated the indignation they were ready to feel. The circus had become a lecture.

The next day Newton and two other persons were installed in the guest suite of Trumbull College, and the students responded to him as they generally do upon meeting celebrities—keeping a respectful distance, being quite careful not to intrude, maintaining a polite reserve—all of which Newton received as a simple lack of hospitality. During the one meal he ate in the college dining hall, for example, Newton turned around in his chair to find a group of students staring at him in open curiosity: he smiled and waved a hand in greeting, as is his custom, whereupon the students, as is their custom, managed a thin, embarrassed smile of their own and bent back over their plates. The warm cordiality of the West had met the cool courtesy of the Ivy League, and by then it was Newton's turn to be disappointed. Nor were matters greatly improved when Newton went to recover his coat and discovered that someone had spat upon it. From the standpoint of an already apprehensive moderator, this was not a promising start.

But the meetings began. It scarcely makes sense to try to characterize them in an introduction like this, but the transcript might be easier to follow if it is noted that Newton walked into the meeting room dressed as he had been the evening before and opened the proceedings by talking for more than an hour about the ideology of the Black Panther Party. His remarks were clearly meant as a formal declaration rather than as a casual introduction, and, as one can readily discern from the record, they were abstract almost to the point of being strenuous. For the rest of the three-hour session, students asked questions —and the first dim outlines of a struggle that would figure throughout the meetings began to appear. The students were trying to lure Newton down from the high cerebral plane he had chosen so he could become the political activist they thought him to be, while Newton had come to discuss ideology and would not be discouraged from doing so. During the whole of that exchange, Erik Erikson made elaborate notes on an artist's pad and said nothing whatever.

Erikson's arrival in New Haven had been a far less dramatic affair. He was a familiar figure around Trumbull College in any case, admired and respected, but hardly a distant stranger. He opened the second session with a lengthy statement of his own, a reflective tour of the territory opened up the day before, and the rhythm of the meetings was becoming established. Newton, the activist, had taken the first risks by stating terms and setting boundaries; Erikson, the thoughtful clinician and professor, had waited to see what ideas and data would be placed on the table so that he could react to them. Erikson's statement, too, was followed by questions from the rest of the participants, but by a drift that seemed almost gravitational in its pull, the questions moved from the center of the discussion to the edge of the table where Newton was sitting. Someone walking into the room might well have thought that a press conference was in progress.

On the third day the discussion wandered from topic to topic and from mood to mood. The shift in topic is reflected clearly enough in the transcript, but the shift in mood is harder to see —the nervousness of the moderators, who sensed a collapse in the project they had engineered; the edginess of Newton, who was clearly disappointed by the apparent indifference of the students to the Seale-Huggins trial occurring not two blocks away; the impatience of the students, who wanted a call to action from these men of words; and all the other irritabilities and anxieties that (had we only remembered) always accompany meetings of this intensity.

The New Haven meetings ended without conclusion, suspended in the middle of one of those shifts in mood.

In closing this account of the New Haven talks, I should probably note that Erikson and Newton, as well as a group of other people connected with the affair, spent a fair amount of time together between the recorded sessions. On the first evening, a small group of us met at the Master's House of Trumbull College to devise something of an agenda. On the second evening, Donald Freed hosted a party for Newton, Charles Garry, and quite a few others. On the third evening, a large gathering of Yale people took place in my home to meet Newton and several of his colleagues—a reception that could fairly be termed "radical chic" of a modest and somewhat academic sort. In between these festivities, there were occasional moments of quiet and earnest talk—not many, but enough to persuade us that our beginnings had been too promising to leave where they were. At the end, we felt ready to talk, so as we parted we talked about a next time.

The transcript of these discussions has been somewhat edited. In the first place, people engaged in earnest talk usually punctuate their utterances and even communicate much of what they want to say through facial expressions, changes in tone, gestures, and so on. In that respect, at least, one needs to edit what one has said *in order* to be faithful to the original, *in order* to reproduce what one remembers having "said" in one form or another. In the second place, discussions like these are repetitious almost as a matter of course, and we have sliced from the transcript those expressions that seem to duplicate each other. In the third place, the transcript of the New Haven meeting was full of the most extraordinary errors. As Erik Erikson notes a little ruefully:

The transcript of the Yale meetings offered more than usual problems to me. In strategic places, there were words which I could not have uttered: for example, I could not have quoted Lincoln as saying, "As I would not be sloth, I would not be monster." His words, of course, were "slave" and "master." But when I read some such absurd passage to myself in my worst accent, it became plausible, say, that "anarchistic" originally was "anachronistic." Quite a difference, though, especially in our context! And if the transcript quotes me as having said, "I'm awfully sorry but I forgot to bring my gun," someone might well wonder what went on at the Yale Press.

A number of persons contributed to the editing process, some of them a good deal more than others, but it is within the general spirit of the undertaking to just mention them in alphabetical order: Herman Blake, Lewis Cole, Kai Erikson, Donald Freed, Sandra Hughes, and Martin Kenner. Both Erik Erikson and Huey Newton have edited their own remarks and reviewed the rest of the text. Questions asked by the various participants at Yale have been edited by Lewis Cole and Kai Erikson with what they hope has been a friendly pencil.

We owe a special debt of gratitude to Elting Morison, who helped plan the New Haven meeting, served as one of its moderators, and would have become one of the editors if time and circumstance had permitted. Chester Kerr, too, assisted the enterprise in many important ways, and we are grateful to him.

Participants in the New Haven meeting, aside from Newton,

Erik Erikson, and the two moderators, were Alan Beller, Samuel Cooper, John Cole, William Horowitz, Sandra Hughes, Caroline Jackson, Vera Jones, Ann Linden, Jennifer Lyman, Donald Mendelsohn, Wayne Neveu, Dwight Raiford, Kurt Schmoke, and Bradley Wong. Voices of the fourteen students and two moderators appear without identification (with one exception noted in the text) because someone misplaced the lists kept during the talks and we were unable to reconstruct who said what from memory.

PART I

Meetings in New Haven

First Day

"Intercommunalism," a Statement by *HUEY P. NEWTON.* Discussion

NEWTON I'll start the discussion by explaining the Black Panther Party's ideology. We believe that everything is in a constant state of change, so we employ a framework of thinking that can put us in touch with the process of change. That is, we believe that the conclusions at which we arrive will always change, but the fundamentals of the method by which we arrive at our conclusions will remain constant. Our ideology, therefore, is the most important part of our thinking.

There are many different ideologies or schools of thought, and all of them start with an a priori set of assumptions. This is because mankind is still limited in its knowledge and finds it hard, at this historical stage, to talk about the very beginning of things and the very end of things without starting from premises that cannot yet be proved.

This is true of both general schools of thought—the idealist and the materialist. The idealists base their thinking on certain presumptions about things of which they have very little knowledge; the materialists like to believe that they are very much in contact with reality, or the real material world, disregarding the fact that they only assume there *is* a material world.

The Black Panther Party has chosen materialist assumptions on which to ground its ideology. This is a purely arbitrary choice. Idealism might be the real happening; we might not be here at all. We don't really know whether we are in Connecticut or in San Francisco, whether we are dreaming and in a dream state, or whether we are awake and in a dream state. Perhaps we are just somewhere in a void; we simply can't be sure. But because the members of the Black Panther Party are materialists, we believe that some day scientists will be able to deliver the information that will give us not only the evidence but the proof that there is a material world and that its genesis was material —motion and matter—not spiritual.

Until that time, however, and for the purposes of this discussion, I merely ask that we agree on the stipulation that a material world exists and develops externally and independently of us all. With this stipulation, we have the foundation for an intelligent dialogue. We *assume* that there is a material world and that it exists and develops independently of us; and we assume that the human organism, through its sensory system, has the ability to observe and analyze that material world.

Now the dialectical materialist believes that everything in existence has fundamental internal contradictions. For example, the African gods south of the Sahara always had at least two heads, one for evil and one for good. Now people create God in their own image, what they think He—for God is always a "He" in patriarchal societies—what He is like or should be. So the African said, in effect: I am both good and evil; good and evil are the two parts of the thing that is me. This is an example of an internal contradiction.

Western societies, though, split up good and evil, placing God up in heaven and the Devil down in hell. Good and evil fight for control over people in Western religions, but they are two entirely different entities. This is an example of an external contradiction.

This struggle of mutually exclusive opposing tendencies within everything that exists explains the observable fact that all things have motion and are in a constant state of transformation. Things transform themselves because while one tendency or force is more dominating than another, change is nonetheless a constant, and at some point the balance will alter and there will be a new qualitative development. New properties will come into existence, qualities that did not altogether exist before. Such qualities cannot be analyzed without understanding the forces struggling within the object in the first place, yet the limitations and determinations of these new qualities are not defined by the forces that created them.

Class conflict develops by the same principles that govern all other phenomena in the material world. In contemporary society, a class that owns property dominates a class that does not own property. There is a class of workers and a class of owners, and because there exists a basic contradiction in the interests of those two classes, they are constantly struggling with one another. Now, because things do not stay the same we can be sure of one thing: the owner will not stay the owner, and the people who are dominated will not stay dominated. We don't know exactly how this will happen, but after we analyze all the other elements of the situation, we can make a few predictions. We can be sure that if we increase the intensity of the struggle, we will reach a point where the equilibrium of forces will change and there will be a qualitative leap into a new situation with a new social equilibrium. I say "leap" because we know from our experience of the physical world that when transformations of this kind occur they do so with great force.

These principles of dialectical development do not represent an iron law that can be applied mechanically to the social process. There are exceptions to those laws of development and transformation, which is why, as dialectical materialists, we emphasize that we must analyze each set of conditions separately and make concrete analyses of concrete conditions in each instance. One cannot always predict the outcome, but one can for the most part gain enough insight to manage the process.

The dialectical method is essentially an ideology, yet we believe that it is superior to other ideologies because it puts us more in contact with what we believe to be the real world; it increases our ability to deal with that world and shape its development and change.

You could easily say, "Well, this method may be successfully applied in one particular instance, but how do you know that it is an infallible guide in all cases?" The answer is that we don't know. We don't say "all cases" or "infallible guide" because we try not to speak in such absolute and inclusive terms. We only say that we have to analyze each instance, that we have found this method the best available in the course of our analyses, and that we think the method will continue to prove itself in the future.

We sometimes have a problem because people do not understand the ideology that Marx and Engels began to develop. People say, "You claim to be Marxists, but did you know that Marx was a racist?" We say, "Well, he probably was a racist: he made a statement once about the marriage of a white woman and a black man, and he called the black man a gorilla or something like that." The Marxists claim he was only kidding and that the statement shows Marx's closeness to the man, but of course that is nonsense. So it does seem that Marx was a racist.

Now if you are a *Marxist*, then Marx's racism affects your own judgment because a Marxist is someone who worships Marx and the thought of Marx. Remember, though, that Marx himself said, "I am not a Marxist." Such Marxists cherish the conclusions which Marx arrived at through his method, but they throw away the method itself—leaving themselves in a totally static posture. That is why most Marxists really are historical materialists: they look to the past to get answers for the future, and that does not work.

If you are a *dialectical materialist*, however, Marx's racism does not matter. You do not believe in the conclusions of one person but in the validity of a mode of thought; and we in the Party, as dialectical materialists, recognize Karl Marx as one of the great contributors to that mode of thought. Whether or not Marx was a racist is irrelevant and immaterial to whether or not the system of thinking he helped develop delivers truths about processes in the material world. And this is true in all disciplines. In every discipline you find people who have distorted visions and are at a low state of consciousness who nonetheless have flashes of insight and produce ideas worth considering. For instance, John B. Watson once stated that his favorite pastime was hunting and hanging niggers, yet he made great forward strides in the analysis and investigation of conditioned responses.

Now that I have said a word about the ideology of the Party, I am going to describe the history of the Party and how we have changed our understanding of the world.

When we started in October 1966, we were what one would call black nationalists. We realized the contradictions in society, the pressure on black people in particular, and we saw that most people in the past had solved some of their problems by forming into nations. We therefore argued that it was rational and logical for us to believe that our sufferings as a people would end when we established a nation of our own, composed of our own people.

But after a while we saw that something was wrong with this resolution of the problem. In the past, nationhood was a fairly easy thing to accomplish. If we look around now, though, we see that the world—the land space, the livable parts as we know them—is pretty well settled. So we realized that to create a new nation we would have to become a dominant faction in this one, and yet the fact that we did not have power was the contradiction that drove us to seek nationhood in the first place. It is an endless circle, you see: to achieve nationhood, we needed to become a dominant force; but to become a dominant force, we needed to be a nation.

So we made a further analysis and found that in order for us to be a dominant force we would at least have to be great in number. So we developed from just plain nationalists or separatist nationalists into revolutionary nationalists. We said that we joined with all of the other people in the world struggling for decolonialization and nationhood, and called ourselves a "dispersed colony" because we did not have the geographical concentration that other so-called colonies had. But we did have black communities throughout the country—San Francisco, Los Angeles, New Haven—and there are many similarities between these communities and the traditional kind of colony. We also thought that if we allied with those other colonies we would have a greater number, a greater chance, a greater force; and that is what we needed, of course, because only force kept us a colonized people.

We saw that it was not only beneficial for us to be revolutionary nationalists but to express our solidarity with those friends who suffered many of the same kind of pressures we suffered. Therefore we changed our self-definitions. We said that we are not only revolutionary nationalists—that is, nationalists who want revolutionary changes in everything, including the economic system the oppressor inflicts upon us—but we are also individuals deeply concerned with the other people of the world and their desires for revolution. In order to show this solidarity, we decided to call ourselves internationalists.

Originally, as I said, we assumed that people could solve a number of their problems by becoming nations, but this conclusion showed our lack of understanding of the world's dialectical development. Our mistake was to assume that the conditions under which people had become nations in the past still existed. To be a nation, one must satisfy certain essential conditions, and if these things do not exist or cannot be created, then it is not possible to be a nation.

In the past, nation-states were usually inhabited by people of a certain ethnic and religious background. They were divided from other people either by a partition of water or a great unoccupied land space. This natural partition gave the nation's dominant class, and the people generally, a certain amount of control over the kinds of political, economic, and social institutions they established. It gave them a certain amount of control over their destiny and their territory. They were secure at least to the extent that they would not be attacked or violated by another nation ten thousand miles away, simply because the means to transport troops that far did not exist. This situation, however, could not last. Technology developed until there was a definite qualitative transformation in the relationships within and between nations.

We know that you cannot change a part of the whole without changing the whole, and vice versa. As technology developed and there was an increase in military capabilities and means of travel and communication, nations began to control other territories, distant from their own. Usually they controlled these other lands by sending administrators and settlers, who would extract labor from the people or resources from the earth—or both. This is the phenomenon we know as colonialism.

The settlers' control over the seized land and people grew to such an extent that it wasn't even necessary for the settler to be present to maintain the system. He went back home. The people were so integrated with the aggressor that their land didn't look like a colony any longer. But because their land didn't look like a free state either, some theorists started to call these lands "neocolonies." Arguments about the precise definition of these entities developed. Are they colonies or not? If they aren't, what are they? The theorists knew that something had happened, but they did not know what it was.

Using the dialectical materialist method, we in the Black

Panther Party saw that the United States was no longer a nation. It was something else; it was more than a nation. It had not only expanded its territorial boundaries, but it had expanded all of its controls as well. We called it an empire. Now at one time the world had an empire in which the conditions of rule were different—the Roman Empire. The difference between the Roman and the American empires is that other nations were able to exist external to and independent of the Roman Empire because their means of exploration, conquest, and control were all relatively limited.

But when we say "empire" today, we mean precisely what we say. An empire is a nation-state that has transformed itself into a power controlling *all* the world's lands and people.

We believe that there are no more colonies or neocolonies. If a people is colonized, it must be possible for them to decolonize and become what they formerly were. But what happens when the raw materials are extracted and labor is exploited within a territory dispersed over the entire globe? When the riches of the whole earth are depleted and used to feed a gigantic industrial machine in the imperialist's home? Then the people and the economy are so integrated into the imperialist empire that it's impossible to "decolonize," to return to the former conditions of existence.

If colonies cannot "decolonize" and return to their original existence as nations, then nations no longer exist. Nor, we believe, will they ever exist again. And since there must be nations for revolutionary nationalism or internationalism to make sense, we decided that we would have to call ourselves something new.

We say that the world today is a dispersed collection of communities. A community is different from a nation. A community is a small unit with a comprehensive collection of institutions that exist to serve a small group of people. And we say further that the struggle in the world today is between the small circle that administers and profits from the empire of the United

States, and the peoples of the world who want to determine their own destinies.

We call this situation intercommunalism. We are now in the age of reactionary intercommunalism, in which a ruling circle, a small group of people, control all other people by using their technology.

At the same time, we say that this technology can solve most of the material contradictions people face, that the material conditions exist that would allow the people of the world to develop a culture that is essentially human and would nurture those things that would allow the people to resolve contradictions in a way that would not cause the mutual slaughter of all of us. The development of such a culture would be revolutionary intercommunalism.

Some communities have begun doing this. They have liberated their territories and have established provisional governments. We recognize them, and say that these governments represent the people of China, North Korea, the people in the liberated zones of South Vietnam, and the people in North Vietnam.

We believe their examples should be followed so that the order of the day would not be reactionary intercommunalism (empire) but revolutionary intercommunalism. The people of the world, that is, must seize power from the small ruling circle and expropriate the expropriators, pull them down from their pinnacle and make them equals, and distribute the fruits of our labor that have been denied us in some equitable way. We know that the machinery to accomplish these tasks exists and we want access to it.

Imperialism has laid the foundation for world communism, and imperialism itself has grown to the point of reactionary intercommunalism because the world is now integrated into one community. The communications revolution, combined with the expansive domination of the American empire, has created the "global village." The peoples of all cultures are under siege by the same forces and they all have access to the same technologies.

There are only differences in degree between what's happening to the blacks here and what's happening to all of the people in the world, including Africans. Their needs are the same and their energy is the same. And the contradictions they suffer will only be resolved when the people establish a revolutionary intercommunalism where they share all the wealth that they produce and live in one world.

The stage of history is set for such a transformation: the technological and administrative base of socialism exists. When the people seize the means of production and all social institutions, then there will be a qualitative leap and a change in the organization of society. It will take time to resolve the contradictions of racism and all kinds of chauvinism; but because the people will control their own social institutions, they will be free to re-create themselves and to establish communism, a stage of human development in which human values will shape the structures of society. At this time the world will be ready for a still higher level, of which we can now know nothing.

I'm through with my talk.

QUESTION   I'm wondering: now that you have established an ideology with which to view the kinds of imperialism going on in the United States, what do you do once the revolution has taken place? What happens once you have taken over the structures made by capitalism and have assumed responsibility for them? Aren't you going to encounter the same struggles between the dominant forms of government and the inferior?

NEWTON   It's not going to be the same because nothing remains the same. All things are in a constant state of transformation, and therefore you will have other contradictions inherent in that new phenomenon. We can be very sure that there will be contradictions after revolutionary intercommunalism is the order of the day, and we can even be sure that there will be contradictions after communism, which is an even higher stage than revolutionary intercommunalism. There will always be contradictions or else everything would stop. So it's not a question of "when the revolution comes": the revolution is always going on. It's not a question of "when the revolution is going to be": the revolution is going on every day, every minute, because the new is always struggling against the old for dominance.

We also say that every determination is a limitation, and every limitation is a determination. This is the struggle of the old and new again, where a thing seems to negate itself. For instance, imperialism negates itself after laying the foundation for communism, and communism will eventually negate itself because of its internal contradictions, and then we'll move to an even higher state. I like to think that we will finally move to a stage called "godliness," where man will know the secrets of the beginning and the end and will have full control of the universe —and when I say the universe, I mean all motion and matter. This is only speculation, of course, because science has not delivered us the answer yet; but we believe that it will in the future.

So of course there will be contradictions in the future. But some contradictions are antagonistic and some contradictions are not antagonistic. Usually when we speak of antagonistic contradictions, we are talking about contradictions that develop from conflicts of economic interest, and we assume that in the future, when the people have power, these antagonistic contradictions will occur less and less.

QUESTION Could you speak to the question of how you are going to expropriate the expropriators when they are the ones with the army and the ones with the police force?

NEWTON Well, all things carry a negative sign as well as a positive sign. That's why we say every determination has a limitation and every limitation has a determination. For example, your organism carries internal contradictions from the moment you are born and begin to deteriorate. First you are an infant, then a small child, then an adolescent, and so on until you are old. We keep developing and burning ourselves out at the same time; we are negating ourselves. And this is just how imperialism is negating itself now. It's moved into a phase we call reactionary intercommunalism and has thus laid the foundation for revolutionary intercommunalism, because as the enemy disperses its troops and controls more and more space, it becomes weaker and weaker, you see. And as they become weaker and weaker, the people become stronger and stronger.

QUESTION   You spoke of technological differences between the various countries of the world. How are you going to integrate all these countries into intercommunalism if these differences exist?

NEWTON   They are already integrated by the mere fact that the ruling circle has control of all of them. Inside the geographical region of North America, for example, you have Wall Street, you have the big plants in Detroit turning out automobiles, and you have Mississippi, where there are no automobile factories. Does that mean that Mississippi is not a part of the complete whole? No, it only means that the expropriators have chosen to put automobile plants in Detroit rather than in Mississippi. Instead of producing automobiles, they grow food in Mississippi that makes stronger the hands of people in Detroit or Wall Street. So the answer to your question is that systems are inclusive: just because you don't have a factory in every single community does not mean that the community is distinct and independent and autonomous, you see.

QUESTION   Well, then, do you see each of the dispersed communities having certain kinds of things to work out among themselves before they can take part in intercommunalism?

NEWTON   They *are* part of intercommunalism, reactionary intercommunalism. What the people have to do is become conscious of this condition. The primary concern of the Black Panther Party is to lift the level of consciousness of the people through theory and practice to the point where they will see exactly what is controlling them and what is oppressing them, and therefore see exactly what has to be done—or at least what the first step is. One of the greatest contributions of Freud was to make people aware that they are controlled much of their lives by their unconscious. He attempted to strip away the veil from the unconscious and make it conscious: that's the first step in feeling free, the first step in exerting control. It seems to be natural for people not to like being controlled. Marx made a similar contribution to human freedom, only he pointed out the *external* things that control people. In order for people to liberate themselves from external controls, they have to know about these controls. Consciousness of the expropriator is necessary for expropriating the expropriator, for throwing off external controls.

QUESTION   So, in the ultimate intercommune, do you see separate, geographically defined communities that have had a specific history and a unique set of experiences? I mean, would each community retain some kind of separate identity?

NEWTON   No, I think that whether we like it or not, dialectics would make it necessary to have a universal identity. If we do not have universal identity, then we will have cultural, racial, and religious chauvinism, the kind of ethnocentrism we have now. So we say that even if in the future there will be some small differences in behavior patterns, different environments would all be a secondary thing. And we struggle for a future in which we will realize that we are all Homo sapiens and have more in common than not. We will be closer together than we are now.

QUESTION   I would like to return to something we were talking about a minute or two ago. It seems to me that the mass media have, in a sense, psychologized many of the people in our country, our own geographical area, so that they come to *desire* the controls that are imposed upon them by the capitalist system. So how are we going to fight this revolution if a great number of people, in this country at least, are in fact psychologically part of the ruling class?

NEWTON   Part of or controlled by?

QUESTION   Well, part of in the psychological sense, because they are not really in power. It's a psychological way of talking about the middle class. Do you have any feelings on that?

NEWTON   First, we have to understand that everything has a material basis, and that our personalities would not exist, what others call our spirit or our mind would not exist, if we were not material organisms. So to understand why some of the victims of the ruling class might identify with the ruling circle, we must look at their material lives; and if we do, we will realize that the same people who identify with the ruling circle are also very unhappy. Their feelings can be compared to those of a child: a child desires to mature so that he can control himself, but he believes he needs the protection of his father to do so. He has conflicting drives. Psychologists would call this conflict neurotic if the child were unable to resolve it.

In a sense, then, that is what we are all about. First, people have to be conscious of the ways they are controlled, then we have to understand the scientific laws involved, and once that is accomplished, we can begin to do what we want—to manipulate phenomena.

QUESTION   But if the opposing forces at this point include a very large number of people, including most of the middle classes, then where will the revolutionary thrust come from?

NEWTON   O.K., I see what you are getting at. That thrust will come from the growing number of what we call "unemployables" in this society. We call blacks and third world people in particular, and poor people in general, "unemployables" because they do not have the skills needed to work in a highly developed technological society. You remember my saying that every society, like every age, contains its opposite: feudalism produced capitalism, which wiped out feudalism, and capitalism produced socialism, which will wipe out capitalism. Now the same is true of reactionary intercommunalism. Technological development creates a large middle class, and the number of workers increases also. The workers are paid a good deal and get many comforts. But the ruling class is still only interested in itself. They might make certain compromises and give a little—as a matter of fact, the ruling circle has even developed something of a social structure or welfare state to keep the opposition down—but as technology develops, the need for workers decreases. It has been estimated that ten years from now only a small percentage of the present work force will be necessary to run the industries. Then what will happen to your worker who is now making four dollars an hour? The working class will be narrowed down, the class of unemployables will grow because it will take more and more skills to operate those machines and fewer people. And as these people become unemployables, they will become more and more alienated; even socialist compromises will not be enough. You will then find an integration between, say, the black unemployable and the white racist hard hat who is not regularly employed and mad at the blacks who he thinks threaten his job. We hope that he will join forces with those people who are already unemployable, but whether he does or not, his material existence will have changed. The proletarian will become the lumpen proletarian. It is this future change—the increase of the lumpen proletariat and the decrease of the proletariat—which makes us say that the lumpen proletariat is the majority and carries the revolutionary banner.

QUESTION   I'd like to ask you a question about the Party. You said that you see the Black Panther Party as primarily a force to educate people, raise their consciousness, end their oppression, and so on. Do you see the Party as educating black people specifically or as educating everybody?

NEWTON   We say that black people are the vanguard of the revolution in this country, and, since no one will be free until the people of America are free, that black people are the vanguard of world revolution. We don't say this in a boasting way. We inherit this legacy primarily because we are the last, you see, and as the saying goes, "The last will be the first."

We believe that black Americans are the first real internationalists; not just the Black Panther Party, but black people who live in America. We are internationalists because we have been internationally dispersed by slavery, and we can easily identify with other people in other cultures. Because of slavery, we never really felt attached to the nation in the same way that the peasant was attached to the soil in Russia. We are always a long way from home.

And, finally, the historical condition of black Americans has led us to be progressive. We've always talked equality, you see, instead of believing that other people must equal us. What we want is not dominance, but for the yoke to be released. We want to live with other people, we don't want to say that we are better: in fact, if we suffer a fault, it is that we tend to feel we are worse than other people because we have been brainwashed to think that way. So these subjective factors, based on the material existence of black people in America, contribute to our vanguard position.

Now as far as the Party is concerned, it has been exclusively black so far. We are thinking about how to deal with the racist situation in America and the reaction black people in America have to racism. We have to get to the black people first because they were carrying the banner first, and we try to do everything possible to get them to relate to us.

QUESTION   You were saying something a while ago about the problem of simplifying your ideology for the masses. Could you say a little more about it?

NEWTON   Yes, that's our big burden. So far I haven't been able to do it well enough to keep from being booed off the stage, but we are learning. I think one way to show how dialectics works is to use practical example after practical example. The reason I am sometimes afraid to do that is that people will take each example and think, "Well, if this is true in one case, then it must be true in all other cases." If they do that, then they become historical materialists like most Marxist scholars and most Marxist parties. These scholars and parties don't really deal in dialectics at all, or else they would know that at this time the revolutionary banner will not be carried by the proletarian class but by the lumpen proletariat.

QUESTION   Talking about contradictions, one of the most obvious contradictions within the black community is the difference in outlook between the black bourgeoisie and the black lower class. How do you raise the level of consciousness in the community to the point where the black bourgeoisie sees its own interests as being the same as those of the lower class?

NEWTON   Well, we are again dealing with attitudes and values that have to be changed. The whole concept of the bourgeoisie—black bourgeoisie—is something of an illusion. It's a fantasy bourgeoisie, and this is true of most of the white bourgeoisie too. There are very few controllers even in the white middle class. They can barely keep their heads above water, they are paying all the bills, living hand-to-mouth, and they have the extra expense of refusing to live like black people, you see. So they are not really controlling anything; they are controlled.

In the same way, I don't recognize the black bourgeoisie as different from any other exploited people. They are living in a fantasy world, and the main thing is to instill consciousness, to point out their real interests, their objective and true interests, just as our white progressive and radical friends have to do in the white community.

QUESTION   How do you go about raising the level of consciousness in the black community? Educationally, I mean. Do you have formal programs of instruction?

NEWTON   Well, we saw a need to formalize education because we didn't believe that a haphazard kind of learning would necessarily bring about the best results. We also saw that the so-called halls of learning did nothing but miseducate us; they either drove us out or kicked us out. They did me both ways. So what we are trying to do is structure an educational institution of our own.

Our first attempt along these lines is what we call our Ideological Institute. So far we have about fifty students, and these fifty students are very—well, may I say very unique students, because all of them are brothers and sisters off the block. What I mean is that they are lumpen proletarians. Most of them are kickouts and dropouts; most of them left school in the eighth, ninth, or tenth grade. And those few who stayed all the way didn't learn how to read or write, just as I didn't learn until I was about sixteen. But now they are dealing with dialectics and they are dealing with science—they study physics and mathematics so that they can understand the universe—and they are learning because they think it is relevant to them now. They will relate this learning back to the community and the community will in turn see the need for our program. It's very practical and relates to the needs of the people in a way that makes them receptive to our teachings and helps open their eyes to the fact that the people are the real power. They are the ones who will bring about change, not us alone. A vanguard is like the head of a spear, the thing that goes first. But what really hurts is the butt of the spear, because even though the head makes the necessary entrance, the back part is what penetrates. Without the butt, a spear is nothing but a toothpick.

QUESTION   What about Malcolm X University? Would you say that it has value?

NEWTON   The whole issue is: who controls? We, the Black Panther Party, control our Ideological Institute. If the people (and when I say "the people" I mean the oppressed people) control Malcolm X University, if they control it without reservation or without having to answer for what is done there or who speaks there, then Malcolm X University is progressive. If that is not the case, then Malcolm X University, or any university by any other name, is not progressive. I like its name, though. [laughter]

QUESTION   The thing I don't understand is: if unity of identity is going to exist in revolutionary intercommunalism, then what will be the contradictions that produce further change? Like, it seems to me that it would be virtually impossible to avoid some contradictions.

NEWTON   I agree with you. You cannot avoid contradictions, you cannot avoid the struggle of opposite tendencies within the same wholes. But I can't tell you what the new opposites will be because they are not in existence yet. See what I mean?

QUESTION   I guess so. But how does all that fit in with your idea of a unified identity?

NEWTON   Well, in the first place, we do not deal in panaceas. The qualitative leap from reactionary intercommunalism to revolutionary intercommunalism will not be the millennium. It will not immediately bring into being either a universal identity or a culture that is essentially human. It will only provide the material base for the development of those tendencies.

When the people seize the means of production, when they seize the mass media and so forth, you will still have racism, you will still have ethnocentrism, you will still have contradictions. But the fact that the people will be in control of all the productive and institutional units of society—not only factories, but the media too—will enable them to start solving these contradictions. It will produce new values, new identities; it will mold a new and essentially human culture as the people resolve old conflicts based on cultural and economic conditions. And at some point, there will be a qualitative change and the people will have transformed revolutionary intercommunalism into communism.

We call it "communism" because at that point in history people will not only control the productive and institutional units of society, but they will also have seized possession of their own subconscious attitudes toward these things; and for the first time in history they will have a more rather than less conscious relationship to the material world—people, plants, books, machines, media, everything—in which they live. They will have power, that is, they will control the phenomena around them and make it act in some desired manner, and they will know their own real desires. The first step in this process is the seizure by the people of their own communities.

Let me say one more thing, though, to get back to your question. I would like to see the kind of communism I just described come into being, and I think it will come into being. But that concept is so far from my comprehension that I couldn't possibly name the contradictions that will exist there, although I am sure that the dialectics will go on. I'll be honest with you. No matter how I read it, I don't understand it.

QUESTION   But I still don't see where the contradictions are going to come in.

NEWTON   I can't see them either because they are not in existence yet. Only the basis for them is in existence, and we can't talk about things in the blue, things we don't know anything about. Philosophers have done that too much already.

QUESTION   You are talking about this ideology of intercommunalism as part of the program of the Black Panther Party and telling us that the idea is to strive for unity of identity. Yet a few minutes ago you mentioned that the Party only accepts blacks as members. That sounds like a contradiction to me.

NEWTON   Well, I guess it is. But to explain it I would have to go back to what I said earlier. We are the spearhead most of the time, and we try not to be too far ahead of the masses of the people, too far ahead of their thinking. We have to understand that most of the people are not ready for many of the things that we talk about.

Now many of our relationships with other groups, such as the white radicals with whom we have formed coalitions, have been criticized by the very people we are trying to help. For example, our offer of troops to the Vietnamese received negative reaction from the people. And I mean from truly oppressed people. Welfare recipients wrote letters saying, "I thought the Party was for us; why do you want to give those dirty Vietnamese our life blood?" I would agree with you and call it a contradiction. But it is a contradiction we are trying to resolve. You see, we are trying to give some therapy, you might say, to our community and lift their consciousness. But first we have to be accepted. If the therapist is not accepted, then he can't deliver the message. We try to do whatever is possible to meet the patient on the grounds that he or she can best relate to, because, after all, they are the issue. So I would say that we are being pragmatic in order to do the job that has to be done, and then, when that job is done, the Black Panther Party will no longer be the *Black* Panther Party.

QUESTION   That brings up a related question in my mind. How do you view the struggles of women and gay people right now? I mean do you see them as an important part of the revolution?

NEWTON   We think it is very important to relate to and understand the causes of the oppression of women and gay people. We can see that there are contradictions between the sexes and between homosexuals and heterosexuals, but we believe that these contradictions should be resolved within the community. Too often, so-called revolutionary vanguards have tried to resolve these contradictions by isolating women and gay people, and, of course, this only means that the revolutionary groups have cut themselves off from one of the most powerful and important forces among the people. We do not believe that the oppression of women or gays will end by the creation of separate communities for either group. We see that as an incorrect idea, just like the idea of a separate nation. If people want to do it, all right; but it won't solve their problems. So we try to show people the correct way to resolve these problems: the vanguard has to include all the people and understand their defects. O.K.?

I'm getting tired. Shall we call it a day?

Second Day

"The Wider Identity," a Statement by *ERIK H. ERIKSON.* Discussion

ERIKSON Yesterday Huey Newton chose to make a comprehensive theoretical and ideological statement which was, in many ways, so foreign to me that I do not really know how to discuss it either as a whole or in detail. So we have agreed that I should make a parallel statement of my own, focusing on those of my terms which Huey Newton referred to yesterday (in his statement and in subsequent conversations) as possible bridges between our ways of thinking. I hope that this may challenge others present to make their positions explicit also.

However, I would rather begin in a more personal vein. It was for me, as it must have been for many of you, a strange and provocative experience to come face to face with Huey Newton —a new (and in years, older) Newton, the radical theorist. I, for one, could not help thinking of my first impression of the earlier (and younger) Newton, the radical activist. So let me reminisce on what had impressed me in what I had read and heard of the younger Newton, the founder of his Party. For it is the man I want to respond to here, not the Party and its vicissitudes. And I say "respond to" with emphasis, since I have heard the word "confrontation" used as a kind of stage direction, which I must repudiate, as I think he must. A few words about his historical role and a very few about myself will show the absurdity of such an expectation.

What to me makes the older and the newer Newton hang together is a certain passionate self-discipline. This was by no means prominent in what the papers chose to report over the years. But it certainly was basic to the way in which Newton helped to create a new self-image for the black man at a time when I would assume that much of the theory of today was probably more latent.

You have all seen the now traditional picture of young Huey Newton like a latter-day American revolutionary with a gun in his hands, held not threateningly, but safely pointing upward. To a man of my age, it was, not too long ago, almost impossible to imagine black men carrying guns openly—black vigilantes, black nightriders in automobiles, keeping an eye on (of all things) the law. Most readers of the news, of course, did not and do not know that according to California law every citizen then had the right to carry a gun, one gun, for self-defense and joint defense. But those who created that law certainly did not envisage anybody but white men doing so, nor did they envisage anybody but potential lawbreakers as the ones to be patrolled by vigilant citizens in an ill-defined and frontier territory.

Now, as some of you know, it is part of my work to interpret phenomena. That is a complex matter and can be embarrassing if the phenomenon in question sits across the table from you. For this reason, too, I must spell out my rationale before we can enter into a discussion of the validity of my interpretations. To interpret, of course, should mean to be objective, beyond approval or condemnation. Yet it is difficult not to admire relevant action at the proper historical moment, and that is what I am talking about.

In my terms, sometimes referred to as "psychohistorical," the point young Newton made, when he was twenty-two, was to show how the black man's territory has never outlived the frontier state and is still the land of undefined laws; and that arbitrary violence in this territory often comes not from roving outlaws but from those charged with the enforcement of the law. Inclined to disregard the rights of black citizens, they break the law under the guise of defending it. He made of the police, then, the symbol of uniformed and armed lawlessness. But he did so by ingeniously turning the white man's own imagery (especially dear to the American West and the Western) around against the white world itself. And in arming himself and his brothers against that world, he emphasized a disciplined adherence to existing law. In fact, he traveled equipped not only with a gun but also with a law book. The book and the fire—it cannot escape us what an elemental pair of symbols this has been in revolts as far removed from each other as that of the Germans in Luther's day and that of the Zionists in our own. It is clear, I hope, that I am here ascribing to Huey Newton certain implicit historical themes which may or may not have been conscious at the time.

Now, historically speaking, it is obvious that in the South, where most of the blacks in the West came from (and where Newton's family came from), it was the nightriders who rode into black territory, once on horseback, now in automobiles. They still do, of course. Quite recently I visited a part of Mississippi where whites still take occasional potshots even at Headstart schools, unable to stomach the fact that blacks are building (admittedly with Northern sympathy and support) true centers of community life.

But a historical deed is not just a matter of turning images around—nor can it be done without an element of great risk, both of excessive violence and of total failure. For behind such images, as I mentioned, there is the matter of *historical identity* —one of the terms I want to clarify today—which reaches deeply into the existence of each community and each individual: and by deeply, I mean into the center of human self-esteem and pride, and thus, in times of danger, of human defensiveness and deadly anger. I know that there have always been black men even in the South who were armed and who used their arms at the risk of having to become fugitives or of being eliminated. But this did not prevent the fact that the communal climate fostered, as it did in other colonialized people, a negative self-image of defenselessness—which became fateful exactly because it became a symbiotic condition for the white Southerner's own sense of superiority. Such symbiotic positives and negatives become a daily and detailed necessity incorporated in every bit of consciousness and in every bit of language and gesture—on both sides. To turn them around, then, and to try to give to the blacks as well as to the police (on the white forefront) transvaluated images means to take enormous risks. Newton and Seale, in fact, maximized this risk by setting the most unorganized and least uniformed ghetto blacks against the most organized and uniformed whites, the police. They reached way down to those strata of young blacks whom even Marx would have considered lumpen proletariat—that is, the "proletariat in rags"—and attempted to bring forth what sense of mutual loyalty and discipline does exist in those who are up against it. To put the police up against these people and then to mark the police as lawless and murderous can, instead of inducing restraints, seem to justify actions on the part of the law which turn into involuntary confessions of lawlessness—as we saw, much later, in the Fred Hampton case. To provoke the law in such a way that the rage unleashed will lead to severe lapses in self-discipline—that, too, can become an implicit if not explicit revolutionary tactic.

Huey Newton's main deed, however, and one powerful reason for the appeal of the Panthers' stance both here and abroad, is in the turning of a negative identity into a positive one, in the sense in which a cornered animal turns on the attacker. This is what the Black Panther imagery stands for, after all. All of this, in part, is a black-and-urban version of a psychic transformation used by the rebellious youth of other colonialized or oppressed people. Eldridge Cleaver even acknowledged at one point a comparison with the Jews of the Diaspora: "Psychologically," he once remarked, black people in America had "precisely the same outlook" as the Eastern European Jews had under Theodor Herzl.

The police and what they stand for thus bore the brunt of a violent transvaluation, while it must be obvious that, man for man, they more or less play (and have played) the role of armed technicians serving on the frontier of the whole society's identity consciousness. Now the success of such a venture—and I am speaking now not of a political victory but of a propagandistic impact way beyond immediate success or failure—depends on the historical moment grasped, as it were, with self-discipline and determination. Historical here means the universal actualization of new images and symbols. And it should be clear that what happened here on the frontier of the Oakland ghetto has its counterpart in the various theaters of war abroad, particularly in Vietnam, where superbly armed and uniformed technicians were again sent to the frontier by a society that wished to preserve the outer borders of an industrial empire. There, too, they have found themselves infuriatingly ineffective against what would seem to them an infiltrating lumpen proletariat. Such guerrilla tactics as were used by "the other side" at first seemed too desperate to be dignified with the term "strategy." But in the long run they worked against overwhelming odds.

This, then, seems to me to be the "actual" background of the theories advanced yesterday by Huey Newton, and I have pointed this out because it is exactly what cannot be so easily seen in what we read in the papers—whether one is talking about our dailies or the Panthers' weekly. Least of all is it apparent in the spasmodic reporting of guerrilla events here or abroad that they represent a new ritualization of warfare. As I have suggested elsewhere, the purpose of ritualization is always that of pointing up the structure of otherwise ambiguous and ambivalent situations; and in the twilight (or should we say darkness) of the social frontier where the lumpen proletariat and the police meet, it may have been important to make implicit hate explicit and let the forefront confront each other hatefully—as a first step toward the transvaluation of ill-defined images that serve only a perpetuation of ambiguity useful to exploiters.

Having gone this far in my interpretation of things, let me go even further and say that such explicitness of irreducible enmity, paired with armed discipline, may be essential not only for systematic violence but also for any hope of subsequent nonviolent solutions. As some of you know, I have recently studied the early life of Mahatma Gandhi, who was a modern nationalist as well as what I would call a religious activist. Now there is a religious element to all true transvaluation of values, especially where it concerns a faith in the God-given gifts of an exile or suppressed people. One might even say that a responsible religious attitude is impossible where one has not first learned to believe in the genius of the people one happens to emerge from: the acceptance of foreign gods whose business it is to favor other skin colors can only lead to a religiosity of meekness and self-debasement. Nor can true humility emerge from humiliation. So Gandhi, too, had to become wholly Indian before he could become a spiritual leader. And there is a relationship between violence and nonviolence which is rarely considered by those who have not studied the question. Gandhi, in fact, is often derided for having believed from time to time in the necessity for his nation to learn universal armed expertise before they could truly denounce the use of arms. The Indian people, you see, have always consisted of a nonmartial majority and an elite of military castes and tribes. So even Gandhi believed at one time that all Indians should learn military discipline. His point was, of course, that nonviolence does not just mean abstention from a violence which one would not have the means to carry through anyway, but the renunciation of armed tactics one would well know how to use. In this sense, the meaningful opposition is not that of arbitrary violence versus fragmented non-violence, but that of disciplined violence versus disciplined non-violence. This is probably even more important among people who, for historical reasons, may be inclined toward unorganized rioting and thus to a diffusion of violence as well as of nonviolent action.

That much about the way I would look at young Newton's early deeds, insofar as I understand them and can see them in the context of my terms and concepts—which is what I proposed to do today.

But while we are dealing with the more personal: can most of us even begin to grasp what this man stands for? Or, to say that again, can anyone really expect a man like him and a man like me to "confront" each other on such issues? While neither he nor I came here with such a purpose in mind, both of us may have our own preconceived ideas as to where and how we may collide once we have established a mutual identification. Yet such identification would not be complete without the acknowledgment of something some of you must have thought when you first contemplated coming here—namely, how impossible it is to claim true empathy with what a man like Huey Newton has gone through since he established what I have been trying to describe. Clinical intuition, human empathy, and warm personal respect (which I certainly feel toward the younger man before me): they each help only a small part of the way. There are at least two kinds of experience which separate men like him from men like me—the experience of violence in a largely hostile world, and the experience of being totally captive, endless days and nights in solitary confinement. Huey has demonstrated a superhuman will under such conditions to keep the body vigorous, the mind alert, and the soul open for new human experience.

But now let me say a word about myself in comparison—or, rather, in contrast.

I am an old psychoanalyst who managed to escape in his

land of origin—and to escape undramatically—either war service
or oppression. Before mass extermination became the rule and
emigration difficult, I came here as what was then still called an
"immigrant," and a favored kind at that, both in occupational
and in racial terms. I know very well that the Nazis would have
categorized me as a Jew and eliminated me if they had caught
me, yet, in the United States at that time, the classification "refugee" had not been invented yet. I still remember that when I
went to register, the woman at the Boston State House said,
"Glad you came." And within a year I had an appointment at
the Harvard Medical School. I "made good" on the wave of success of my field. Now it was very generous of Huey to refer to
me as a "fellow dropout" from college,* a designation as meaningful to me as any honorary degree, but it should be remembered that I was one of those favored dropouts to whom lack of
involvement in traditional academic terms meant an easier commitment to a revolutionary new school of thought. I mean, of
course, psychoanalysis—and if I call it revolutionary in its origins, I mean more than a radical turn in psychological thought.
I mean that Freud was a revolutionary doctor in that he dared
to go against his whole profession and to free a whole "class" of
people, the mentally ill (then considered constitutionally inferior), from systematic prejudice. More, he showed that prejudice itself, like any other kind of enforced inferiority, owes its
power to the fact that it helped other people (here the "normal"
majority) to overlook in themselves vulnerabilities and conflicts
which they had attempted to "drive into" those poor devils, the
diagnosed patients. But he did something else which really goes
to the very core of revolutionary change: he showed that man,
throughout history, has bought his own adulthood not only by
exercising his maturing faculties but by alienating himself from
the child in himself. He showed that man is born not only with
a great variety of gifts but also a potentially perverse variability

* In a passage not recorded on tape, Newton had noted that neither he
nor Erikson had finished college. (Ed.)

of drives, which, through a prolonged childhood, are tamed and adjusted to a particular style of adulthood—mostly by the imposition of irrational guilt. Childhood, then, is the model of all oppression and enslavement, a kind of inner colonialization, which forces grown-ups to accept inner repression and self-restriction. In fact, outer colonialization probably would never have been possible without the inner one, by which (as I once tried to show) a negative identity is imposed on the colonialized and with it a certain repository of self-hate. This, in turn, can be used by the exploiting class or race or sex for its self-aggrandizement and for the projection of its own self-hate. In this sense, Freud's and Marx's revolutionary ideas complement each other. The young Freud dreamed of politics, and the young Marx certainly developed the idea of unconscious motives, if determined by material conditions. For did not Marx, in calling for a militant class consciousness, also imply a class unconscious? Surely when we wake up in the morning and think like members of a ruling class or as citizens of an imperialist country, we do not decide to do so with a conscious intent: we are part of a largely unconscious conspiracy of maintaining a collective image of reality composed pretty much in equal measure of clear facts, debatable opinions, and outright delusions. And so, as I have pointed out, does the exploited class or race accept a "reality" daily enforced by the media serving those in power—which is exactly why revolutions have to be shocking in order to really unhinge existing identities. In this sense, it seems to me, Marx's class consciousness, too, calls for the determination of becoming conscious of something that festers in the unconscious until it is realized, systematized, and put to work with deliberation.

I might add that in Vienna, in the early years, psychoanalysis was a kind of psychiatric underground, quite at odds with the official academic world. Freud himself never became what would be called a full professor or chairman of a department here—all of which must seem improbable to some of you now. But what happens to a revolutionary idea when it becomes

prosperous—that is quite another matter. Originally, psychoanalysis, like any revolutionary transvaluation, aroused resist-
ances (if, by its very nature, often more disguised ones), for to
accept psychoanalytic insights means to realize some of the unconscious foundations on which our own hard-won identities
rest, and it means to gain insight at the cost of any traditional
claim to superiority. And this, in turn, not only arouses anxiety;
it arouses irrational rage such as is still quite common today
wherever men (and women!) are suddenly faced with the
mere probability that both their unfreedom and their search
for liberation may, in addition to a clear social rationale, have
unconscious determinants also. All this is a natural by-product
of the overwhelming fact that man is a conscious animal—and
mighty proud of it. Nevertheless, whatever man in a given period of history represses with special vengeance has marked
historical determinants. The very origin of Freud's psychoanalysis is linked to that special sexual repression which characterized the Victorian age and its literally sickening insistence on
the "purity" of children and of women (and especially of la-
dies), the very cause of widespread hysteria. But the symptoms and the inner processes that come to be understood in
one period of history must be traced into the succeeding ones
and related to what becomes more obvious then. I have pointed
out that the struggle for a modern identity ("the self-made
man") and against an array of negative identities is both the
inner and the outer struggle dominant today.

As I try to point up the revolutionary element in the origins
of my field, I may be trying to tell you of my own involve-
ments at the age Huey is now. Maybe I mean to say: one revolution is enough for one person. And it is true enough that I
have not found a genuine occasion for revolutionary activism
in my life. But I do believe that Huey's activism as well as his
educational goals touch on our work exactly in the area of
childhood as the very ground of both the suppression of potentials and the repression of will—and, by the same token, of true

hope. That is why I emphasized the transvaluation of identity which Newton's revolutionary deed may imply for generations of young blacks.

Here is where we touch, although I know from a private conversation we had last night that Huey had some objections to the way I first wrote such things up in *Childhood and Society*. Let me repeat here what I said to him. I asked him to remember that my first book was written during the Roosevelt era, when the whole American enterprise, foreign and domestic, seemed to be going in a very different direction, an antitotalitarian and antiracist direction, especially in the eyes of a recent immigrant. Only much later, and only when some young people put their lives on the line, could we, too, fully perceive the fact that we had largely overlooked the fate of the black citizenry who were kept in their place so as to constitute what slaves always meant besides cheap labor—the inferior identity to be superior to. But I must also say that immigrants like myself came to this country without any childhood-conditioned awareness of skin color—a fact which made us believe at first that Americans must be on the way to overcoming this historical childhood disease.

That much for mutual identification—for now. But where (if he will be patient with this kind of thing a little while longer) do I see the old Newton in the new one? When Huey mentioned education yesterday, I couldn't help remembering that sovereign statement by William James: "The first course in psychology I ever took was the first one I ever taught." There was a dropout for you who came back with a vengeance! He learned by teaching. And what we saw yesterday was an example of one who acts, learns, and teaches in even measure.

But I guess neither confession nor flattery will help me to avoid taking a stand on what Huey said yesterday. And taking a stand here means first of all to admit that I did not understand much of it. I am not trained in dialectics: when it comes to a formulation such as that reality exists independently of all

of us, I would just be inclined to say, sure, that is the basis of
all scientific search—to find what can be agreed upon as physi-
cally existing, consensually provable, and mathematically de-
monstrable. Freud, too, began as a physiologist, and his whole
theory of drives was based on the attempt to explain—or at
any rate the hope of being able to explain one day—man's motives on the basis of the nervous stuff we are made of. This
medical materialism, however, has also led to a pseudomateri-
alism by which it was attempted to reduce the richest motiva-
tional data to physiological processes which were not de-
monstrable. My generation had to try to build a bridge, then,
between the medical-psychiatric and the social-developmental
facts in man's life. And there, my own daily work would lead
me to focus on the fact that what is called material reality at a
given historical time may still, on the whole, be dependent as
much on what we *wish* to have true as on what we *know* to be
true. I would say, in fact, that Marx as well as Freud showed
up systematically the unconscious ways in which highly intelligent people can bend "realities" to political and philosophical
imagination. But even such insight is historically relative and
must go on becoming historically conscious. This is one reason
why, about a decade ago, I interrupted both my practice and
my teaching of psychoanalysis in order to do historical studies.
I felt that we tended to adjust future practitioners to a conceptual system which first had to learn to become historically
self-conscious.

So I am very much preoccupied now with historical relativity—for example, such a seemingly simple fact that the sky is
above my head can mean different things to different people at
different times. I think of the sky's position in the wide hori-
zons of American Indians. I think of Kant, the German who
linked the sky above us with the moral law within us. And I
think of those astronauts out there and how *our* experience of
the sky above us is not only being turned around but also polit-
icized. Our immediate image of the world is shrinking in the

face of the infinite solar systems around us, and yet it is possible for an American president to call the moment when he speaks to the men on the moon (valiant technicians to be sure) the greatest moment in history, forgetting Golgotha along with all other stages of the drama of man's freedom. Success is all. What I probably want to say is, simply, it is given to us to analyze concrete conditions concretely, we must also be aware of our tendency to combine what we have recognized as concrete in a total ideological image which has political as well as educational consequences.

This brings me to intercommunalism and its possible relation to another set of terms of mine—pseudospecies. I first used this term in a discussion in London, where Konrad Lorenz heard it and subsequently ascribed to me the very useful term "pseudo-speciation." This means not only that man has never quite realized his identity as a species, but also that groups of men have made transitory and spurious attempts at *making like* a species. This first became obvious to me when, as a young psychoanalyst, I set out to study and compare two American Indian tribes at a time when it was still fashionable to liken collective "primitive" idiosyncrasies to the "neurotic" symptoms of "civilized" individuals like you and me. The Sioux Indians hunting buffalo and the Yurok Indians fishing salmon had built around the central fact of their material (or what we would today call ecological) relationship to one segment of nature, a totally different world-image with its own cosmology and history. And there was no mistaking it—each of them made like *the real people* and called themselves just that, implying that others were not quite the real people. Now, the term "pseudo," which can mean anything from "illusory" to "counterfeit," could imply that man is the biggest liar in the universe. This could hardly be disproven, since he is the one who invented both truth and falsehood, both sincerity and make-believe. At the same time, he is the animal with a history, which means that he will periodically kill other people for the purpose of a new truth replacing another in the defense of which he had killed other people a short time before. So this ethnocentrism and spurious specieshood is also the greatest obstacle in the creation of a truly universal sense of being "the people." All this seems related to Marx's insistence that the history of man is that of a species which must as yet find itself by revolutionary steps of becoming more conscious of its own specieshood. Such ideas have assumed today a certain power among the young who realize as never before what it *may* mean to be a "human being" rather than a creature forced into national, racial, and religious identities and technical and role specializations not of their own choosing—or, at any rate, not conducive to a sense of identity. It is here where world youth suddenly unnerves us all by behaving and dressing and talking like some kind of new species (almost a pseudopseudospecies) making a hostile or inferior species of all those who based their identities on previous pseudospecies and on the hate and fear of otherness in regions, neighborhoods, and even families. And yet, you can also see how a new kind of people must call another kind names (such as "pigs") with a hate which can be murderous and provocative of murder. But at least the new division into an old and a young species upsets all previous divisions, and since all the young will be older together, this new division has built-in correctives.

You can see now why I was especially interested in Huey's discussion of the nationalist phase in his thinking and on the difference between the revolutionary-nationalist and internationalist-revolutionary stance. For his search here seems to correspond and give direction to a universal necessity to overcome existing pseudospecies mentalities and to redefine both the widest possible sense of communality and the smallest viable communities.

In my terms, I would say that the biggest problem facing a universal "people" today is the question of how wide an identity one can afford without becoming formless, ineffective, and lost, and how small must and can be genuine communalities, concrete living situations in which a wider identity finds its home in the here and the now. And if the formulation of any revolutionary idea must always be based on a powerfully dormant or already awakening new consciousness, I would again refer both to the world-wide identifications in modern youth and to its often desperate search for new forms of intimacy and closeness in interpersonal and communal ways. At any rate, that some young Americans and Japanese, French and Germans, feel closer to one another than they feel to their parent generations, who so recently made war on each other, is a highly hopeful sign. It means that a new revolutionary spirit can count on a common technology and communication, a joint fund of information and education, all transcending mutual nationalist isolation and the corporate structures of their individual societies. What holds them together is both the sense of a world community interconnected by technological means and a sense of an immediate if sometimes passing community not larger than a concrete, visible, and touchable circle of individuals. This, somehow, will be the basic dialectics of a culture of the future, and I daresay that social structure, architectural design, and political organization must sooner or later adapt to it.

But what does all this have to do with intercommunalism, what with that ubiquitous phrase "human beings," and what with a new "consciousness"—the last two, incidentally, being implicitly reactionary concepts insofar as they assume as already given what must be struggled for in detailed and sometimes shocking ways? And most of all with a deep responsibility for the next generation already concretely about us: the future, it seems, is so often sacrificed to the rhetoric of an immediate sense of liberation which often is nothing but what I would call an indefinite moratorium, an indefinite delay of adult responsibility. We will, therefore, be intensely interested in Huey Newton's neighborhood activities, and in his educational philosophy. What he calls reactionary intercommunalism may, on the other hand, have to do with the persistent danger that people will always again be divided into new kinds of pseudospecies which defiantly uphold their "inborn" or "earned" right to consider themselves the dominant species on earth—even, it seems, rights once earned through revolutions and liberations.

Would you like to interrupt me here? Or shall I go on and say one more word which may *really* be my conclusion? It is about the United States, which has brought together such people as us—immigrants and descendants of immigrants, blacks and descendants of slaves—which is to say both people with a maximum sense of having been free to come here and people with a maximum sense of having been forced to come here and having remained unfree. Nothing could divide the respective identities of different people more than the sense of free choice and the sense of being without it; and yet, by the mere dialectics of living here for generations, does not the American black "belong" here more than anywhere else?

Now what, then, *does* the American identity stand for? As you know, for the longest time this country has prided itself, beside technical know-how, on having a "way of life." To be an American citizen meant first of all to be part of a wider identity than any of the constituent identities brought along by the immigrants. But this wider identity improvised and sported by the first second generation still was balanced by a communal life of great intensity, often clustered around the original immigrants or, for that matter, the migrants to the West. But the American identity was always characterized by an openness toward the future, by an emphasis on what each individual and each group might yet become—and not on where it came from or what it was. This resulted in what to other countries appeared to be an adolescent stance, as if Americans felt that an all too early and all too well defined adulthood meant to look too much like the immigrant parents. In the meantime, it was the women's job to keep "the boys" in line. It was the readiness to *re*adjust and to start *anew* that was the test of character for many. This, of course, happened to fit the spread of the industrial civilization on this vast continent—the very civilization which America, when it became an empire, imported into the old countries and especially to our former enemies.

Incidentally, is "empire" the right word? It conjures up the Roman Empire or the British Empire, and having just studied the way Gandhi, the separatist within that empire, became a nationalist and internationalist, I would rather call America a World Technocracy which imports to her world markets also a technocratic identity. And that identity, before our eyes and within ourselves, has become so standardized, so role-determined, so bureaucratized, that the stance of making like a forever new kind of people turns at times into a caricature, not related anymore to concrete conditions. But, at the end, the British Empire in a dialectical way served the emergence of new nations by first forcing them into subjugation and then tempering it with a kind of identity as members of the empire. It thus showed them the way to rebellion and a new national identity. Similarly, I feel, this country may prove to have served the emergence of new communal images, based, in the last analysis, on what the immigrants came here for in the first place.

That is exactly what makes the identity of our black citizens so central to the future of America *and* to that of a wider identity anywhere. For as America exports its dreams along with its goods, it must admit that it failed to share the same goods and the same dreams with those whom it forced to come here and whom it forced to serve those in power. Yet, as we said, nobody can really find his most adult identity by denying it to others; nor, for that matter, can those who were denied that identity find it by seeking another communality, unless it be one that transcends as well as embraces the old one.

So we will be interested in knowing what kind of world organization you foresee for your intercommunalism. What will be the smallest units and what the largest? And if I may end with a question which interests me right now to the point that I go around like Diogenes with a flashlight, what kind of adult, what kind of mature citizen, do you visualize as the intercommunalist? I know that we have been so preoccupied with the sons who want to kill their fathers that we have failed to take a really good look at the fathers who, always again, sacrifice their sons, who cast gods into the images of superfathers so that they will sanction the sacrifices of the sons. Maybe the adult partaking in a world-wide identity will need neither a father-image nor a god figure in that compensatory sense, but only an ideal of maturity as the symbolic guarantor of a universal adulthood. This, too, we must discuss in historical perspective.

I talked a long time, but then so did you!

NEWTON I'd like to say that I cannot really see what Erik meant when he talked about the old Huey Newton and the new Huey Newton, and maybe that is because I'm new to Erik and the other people here. I'm the same old thing—not really the same old thing, because I'm in a constant state of transformation just as everything else is—but I don't think there has been any kind of qualitative leap, any real change. Let me clarify something.

The Black Panther Party was formed in 1966, and at that time, as I mentioned yesterday, we thought of ourselves as nationalists. Now prior to 1966 I had been involved in many organizations and parties—the Black Muslims, for example, even though I did not join because I could never quite accept the mystical or religious aspect of it. But there were other organizations too. And even from the beginning I found it difficult to accept some of the black nationalist ways: I tried to develop an attitude of great hatred for people, in this instance white people, and every time I thought I had that attitude all devel-

oped and internalized, my comrades would call me on the car-
pet about something. For example, sometimes I would do
courteous things such as opening a door for a woman who
happened to be white, and they would ask me why I had done
that. When I did these things I would be criticized; but when
I didn't do these things, I would feel a certain guilt about it.
And I really felt that I should have hatred for all of these people generally because all of them had received some privileges
from the fact that their foreparents had been robbers and rap-
ists and so on.

I mention these personal things to give you some background. The Black Panther Party, from its very conception,
was meant as an antiracist party. Even with our rhetoric, we
made it very clear that we were fighting against racism, that
the purpose of our organization was to transform things so that
racism would no longer exist and no longer affect us. I say this
because Erik seems to think that the Party found it necessary
to even hate some people at this stage in its development.
There is something to that, of course, but I would like to point
out one thing about hate. Love and hate are not opposites;
they are on the same pole, and the opposite of both love and
hate is indifference. It's difficult for a black person in America
to be indifferent, so you can imagine the kind of agony one
goes through. It is difficult to be indifferent, but it is also difficult to love, you see. To be involved often means to hate, but
because love and hate both grow from the same pole, there's
love there too.

Now, of course, the Black Panther Party is not based upon
hate. We feel that our revolutionary program must be guided
by a feeling of love—armed love we sometimes call it. I don't
like to use the word "love" again, but the language is poor:
maybe there should be a new word to express what I mean
about involvement and acceptance.

QUESTION   I would like to raise something which has always been a source of deep personal conflict for me. I look at

the United States and the ruling structure, and I do not like it. I do not like the violence and oppression I see here and in Vietnam and in practically every other country. Now I can see in an intellectual way that the only way to react against this violence is with more violence. But when I read the Panther paper and see words like "shoot to kill," well, I just can't relate to that either. So would you speak to the question of wanting to create a new world and a new universal humanity, and at the same time having to pick up a gun and shoot?

NEWTON Well, as I said yesterday, the Black Panther Party is against violence and works for the day when it will no longer be necessary. We want to abolish all guns and all wars because we believe it is better for people to resolve their differences without violence. But we are not idealists, and because we are not idealists we try to understand things in their material context. And until the actual conditions exist where defense with a gun is not necessary, we have to act appropriately. It is insane to ask the Vietnamese to lay down their guns when the American ruling circle is napalming them. It is insane to ask the underground operating in South Africa to put down their guns when blacks there are treated like slaves. It is insane because you are asking people to suffer materially for an ideal that will not benefit them.

So we condemn violence, but we make a distinction between the violence of the aggressor and the self-defense of the people. During the years of slavery, for example, the slave master kidnapped people, split up their families, forced them to labor, shipped, tortured, and killed them, stole all the profit from their work. This was the actual material condition of their lives. So if the slaves revolted—and they did, many times —they were defending themselves against murder. This is what Frederick Douglass meant when he said (let me read this): "The slave is fully justified in helping himself to the gold and silver, and the best apparel of his master . . . Such taking is not stealing in any sense of the word. . . . Slave holders had made it almost impossible for the slave to commit any crime known to the laws of God or to the laws of man. If he steals, he takes his own; if he kills, he imitates only the heroes of the Revolution." We translate that to mean that oppressors have no rights which the oppressed are bound to respect.

So we believe that people have to defend themselves: that is why we armed ourselves openly when we started the Party. We took this risk because we felt that the people had to be educated about the potential power of the armed black community; and now that the example has been made, we are concentrating on helping the people develop things they will want to protect—the survival programs.

You see, Chairman Mao's quote that "political power grows out of the barrel of a gun" is misunderstood time and time again. Most people interpret this to mean that political power *is* a gun, but that's not the point. The verb in the sentence is "grows": political power *grows* from the barrel of a gun; it culminates in the people's ownership and control of the land and the institutions thereon. Mao's own practice shows this: he was not interested in spreading the Communists' influence through mobile guerrilla units, but he believed deeply in establishing political power.

So we believe that in order to get rid of the gun, it is necessary to pick it up. We believe that material conditions produce the violence of the aggressor and the self-defense of the victim, and that the people have a right and an obligation to resist attack upon their attempts to change the material conditions of their lives.

QUESTION   Maybe I feel that way in part because I have never had a gun picked up against me, but ...

NEWTON   No, you haven't, because you are protected by the police and by the imperial army.

QUESTION   All right, part of my hang-up about picking up a gun is that I have never had it picked up against me. But what bothers me the most is this: I can see that the North Vietnamese people need their guns, but when I read the Panther paper I get the impression that it is indifferent to those people who have been killed. I mean the paper sometimes strikes me as a sort of scorecard.

NEWTON   Well, you know, the Vietnamese also shoot down airplanes. I have a ring at home made from an American airplane that was cut down over North Vietnam while attempting to bomb the Vietnamese with napalm and TNT. The Vietnamese use all the little scraps of the planes they cut down to make rings, and then they give these rings to their friends. Imprinted on the ring is the number of planes they have destroyed: I think the one I have has the number 1300 on it. We are very proud of the ring because we are proud that they are able to defend themselves with primitive weapons. They have even shot down helicopters with rifles.

But after the plane falls, the Vietnamese take the dead pilot and bury him, making sure to put flowers on his grave. According to one account I read, a reporter saw this happen and asked the people why they put flowers on the pilot's grave, considering that he was destroying their children and villages. And they answered that the pilot was a victim, an unconscious lackey of the ruling circle. The reporter said that when the Vietnamese down a plane, they weep for the victim and preserve his grave so that when the war is over his people can come and take him home.

We feel the same way. We have great compassion for people, and we really believe that the death of any person diminishes us because we are involved in mankind. But we will not hesitate to use whatever force is necessary so that sanity might prevail and people keep their dignity.

You mentioned "universal identity" a little while ago. You know, it is interesting that when we were talking last night, the professor stated it was difficult for him, even though he is an immigrant like myself, to understand what I have been through. But I think that I, or most black people, can understand the suffering the professor went through. Black people can understand it because they have always been rejected in this country. We have never felt that this country was our home, and our internalization of Western values had made it impossible for us to feel at ease in Africa. Even knowing this, we are still nostalgic much of the time and feel that we would rather deal with the many cultural differences one finds in Africa than deal with the racism and exploitation here. But then we realize that the Africans are catching as much hell as any people in the world, and from the same controller, too. Like the saying goes, I went to the mountain to hide my face, but the mountain cried out, "No hiding place." We cannot hide. So out of this experience of suffering and oppression, the Party tries to develop something of a universal identity.

You know, I stayed in solitary confinement for three years, and just before I got out they took me from the state penitentiary and put me back in the county jail on what they call "little death row." I had stayed on little death row for a month and a half before I was shipped to the isolation cell. There had been five people there then, all of them people the authorities expected to go to the gas chamber. And when I was returned there, prior to my release, two of the guys were still there, one of them black and one of them white. They had gotten reversals too, but they had already gone through their second trials and had been sentenced to death again.

I felt alienated for the first time since being in prison, very alone and very sad. The first time, they were all going to death and I was going to jail, but now they were going to death and I was being released. I wanted to apologize to them for being released, even though I had to go through a second trial too, because why should I have been released while they were going to the death chamber? Why should the people have demanded my release and not theirs? Because of my identification with those men, I wasn't really released from prison: until every one of them is out of the death cells, I'll still be there.

And it is the same with the world. Unless we cultivate an identity with everyone, we will not have peace in the world.

ERIKSON We certainly could stop with what you said right now, but I have to make it clear that when I referred to my status as an immigrant, I really meant to emphasize the opposite from what you inferred—especially when one considers how many immigrants have suffered profoundly. I did not suffer at all, except to the extent that one can get mighty anxious when one arrives here with a young family. I will never forget the moment when our ship first sighted that coldly competitive skyline of New York. The sight more or less puts you in a mental state of survivorship, both in the sense of having to accept, without looking back too much, the fact of your own survival abroad, and in the sense of being determined to survive as a family here, too. All this at first narrows your perceptiveness and, I'm afraid, your capacity to empathize with the struggling masses, until you have gained a foothold and a self-definition as American. And, as I said, I happened to be one of the select immigrants who comes with the right kind of professional equipment and, therefore, is given a special chance, and, in addition, is made to feel that he is bringing an alleviative technique needed for medical progress and progress in general. It was only when, in my clinical work, I found social interpretations inescapable, that I slowly became aware of the depth and cruelty of the social conflicts in this country.

QUESTION I hate to bring up the idea, but it is totally possible and maybe even best that a revolution happen in my lifetime so that my children will benefit from it. But it deeply concerns me at the same time, because whether I choose to be a part of it or not—I am black and my children will be involved—I will be the target of some retaliation. And the retaliation that may come will probably be similar to that which happened in Austria or Germany when the Gestapo routed out the Jews. It's all a matter of position. All black people in the United States will be part of whatever happens. But how in your view do we raise our children or prepare them to be ready for this type of reaction? It's a bad question, but you see my confusion. We know that something is going to happen, whether it is started by the Black Panther Party or someone else, and whatever happens we will be a part of it.

NEWTON   Yes, you will be part of it because everything is interconnected; and no matter how much they would like to, white people cannot run away from it either because they are definitely involved as a part of the species.

QUESTION   But in this country right now we are in the minority.

NEWTON   Yes, but there is only one world community. In the context of this country, we are a minority; but in the context of the empire, we are definitely a majority. We do not say this to give people hope but to show them the true nature of the world today.

We can set the best example for our children by showing them how to love and how to fight against things that jeopardize the freedom of the people. In spite of the racism in this country, in spite of the history of oppression against us, we have to show our children how to love and how to defend ourselves. The only way the people of the world can resolve the contradiction between love and defense is to reverse the dominance, at which point we can keep the love and get rid of the gun. This is why we talk in our paper about people exerting their power. We have been conditioned to believe that we should not defend ourselves, even though fifty million of us have been killed in this country; we have been taught that we should be very humble and act like little Jesuses.

Well, we do not accept that idealism. We accept things the way they are. The oppressed peoples of the world are only children now; they are children because they do not have power and do not control phenomena. For many thousands of years they were hardly recognized at all, except as the toiling masses; and it is only now, as Fidel says, that they are beginning to write their own history. As children, they would be wiped out like the Jews in the ghettoes of Nazi Germany; but as mature adults, they would take the way of the Jews in the Warsaw ghetto and keep their human dignity.

This is the conviction of the Party. We know that the people have to have control or else the people will always be children. The people must express their will to power, and we believe that their desire to do so is beyond good and evil.

QUESTION Much of the impact of the Black Panther Party, and the focus of much of the criticism of the Party, has been your willingness to come out and say that you are prepared to defend yourselves. Some people say: Look, if you are truly revolutionary, then you shouldn't play your trump card by telling people what you are going to do, because then they are going to pick you off one by one.

NEWTON You are now talking about strategy. Uncle Ho said that it is incorrect to publicize military strategy for military reasons, but that it is perfectly correct to publicize military strategy for political reasons. To judge the correctness of our actions, then, you must understand what we were trying to do.

We believe that only the people can expropriate power from the ruling circle here and bring about the necessary transition in the world. So our primary task has been to change the attitude of the people toward that power. Helplessness in the face of oppression is the first attitude that has to be changed, because the slave never expropriates power from the master until he realizes that the master is not God and is not bulletproof. And then it is necessary to teach the people that they do not have to accept life at the cost of the loss of their dignity, and the only way to do this is to offer them examples of people who say if they cannot be free, then they will die trying.

We no longer go around with bandoliers and guns because we believe we have helped change that attitude. If we had never offered them an example like that, though, they would

not know us now; we would never have become their true representatives and leaders. Now we are opening up a new front,
speaking out and saying that we might do something to the
slave master. We are put into jail for that. We are murdered in
our sleep, as Fred Hampton was. We are framed, as Bobby
and Ericka were. This goes on. But at the same time these acts
have gained us the attention of the people, and the vanguard
that does not have the attention of the people has no way of
challenging their unconscious state.

MODERATOR   We have been at it three hours now. Let's
break and see where we are tomorrow.

Third Day

General Discussion

MODERATOR All right, here we go. I sense a burning question over there.

QUESTION I have a question I'd like both of the main participants to speak to. In talking about this conference beforehand, I got the impression that this was going to be a confrontation between, you know, two distinguished people in the public eye. And it really has not been that at all. I would just like to know why you are participating in this.

NEWTON Well, I guess I should say first that I was very interested in getting a chance to talk to Mr. Erikson and to the rest of you. And of course a book may come out of this encounter, and the Black Panther Party will need the funds if we are fortunate enough to get any. So I am largely here to exploit the situation—and to exploit the students too, I guess. That's why.

ERIKSON I don't know what I can add to that. Huey left me out of the category of those he claims he is exploiting. I certainly wanted to meet him, although I was never a party to any attempt to make this a confrontation between two people. I should add that I am somewhat disappointed that the moderators have taken their impartial roles so seriously that so far they have not asserted their own fields: I think that a political statement and a psychological statement need to be bridged by some discussion of social structure and of historical process. But I will also say, since you ask me directly, that I would not have come here if the students had not been here too. Their comments on the nature of our presentations are very basic to the whole meeting.

QUESTION   I have a burning question, too, for Mr. Newton. I have been reading over some of the notes I have taken and, frankly, I really cannot find anything that's startling or new about revolutionary intercommunalism. It seems to me that the ideology is old. It substitutes new terms for old.

NEWTON   The *phenomenon* is new. It did not exist before.

QUESTION   But it really seems like a visionary ideology for such a materialist as you and almost impractical.

NEWTON   You mean materialism is visionary?

QUESTION   No, no, that's not what I'm saying. I'm saying that this whole thing about a unified identity is visionary. You are saying that the whole world is linked and is reacting in a certain way to the American empire, and this seems to me a repeat of something that has been said before. So I am wondering why you think the notion is really new.

NEWTON   First of all, the Party does not steal ideas. It often synthesizes ideas and tries to put them into practice, which gives us a deeper understanding of the original idea. So maybe you should direct your question to Mr. Erikson, because he . . .

ERIKSON   He steals ideas? [laughter]

NEWTON   No, no. But his subject is identity. He is talking about a universal identity; I am talking about a culture that is essentially human; and I am merely trying to show the relationship and the similarity between those two approaches.

QUESTION   I understand that Mr. Erikson should address himself to that point from a psychological perspective. But since the Party is supposed to have a program that will bring about this concept of intercommunalism, it should also take into consideration that . . .

NEWTON   Excuse me, but you are missing the point. We are not bringing about the concept of intercommunalism or even the fact of intercommunalism. Reactionary intercommunalism, which is the order of the day, was brought about by the ruling circles of American imperialism. I am just describing an actual system of relationships in the world today.

QUESTION   Then what approach does the Party take to intercommunalism. How do you relate to that fact?

NEWTON   We see ourselves as among the victims of reactionary intercommunalism. As victims, we resist; as materialists, we try to understand what our situation is in respect to it. We try to relate to it, therefore, by educating the people to their real condition and engaging them in actions that will change that condition. We try to find out what reactionary intercommunalism is and then try to manipulate it in the people's favor.

QUESTION   How are you going to manipulate it? In what direction?

NEWTON   Well, the people of the world are manipulating it already by struggling against reactionary intercommunalism. There are battlefronts throughout Asia, Africa, Latin America, and there is turmoil in Europe now too. People are dissatisfied with the state of the world today and they are resisting.

And all of these struggles are against the American ruling circle in one way or another. Mozambique and Angola, for example, belong to Portugal, and liberation fronts are fighting in both places. But the Portuguese belong to NATO and Americans supply them with the weapons they use to enslave the Africans.

QUESTION   I think you may be a materialist, but it seems to me that you are not dealing with material conditions. You are dealing with a grand scheme which does not relate to me at all in a practical sense. I don't think anyone denies that there are dissatisfied people in the world trying to do something about their lot, but what we are interested in is getting more specific feedback about what is going on here with the Panthers in this country.

NEWTON   You say you are concerned about the people in

this country, but I would speculate that you are concerned about a particular group of people in this country. You keep saying, "Let's not talk about the Vietnamese, let's not talk about the people in Angola and Mozambique, let's not talk about Ericka and Bobby or any of the sufferings of the people. Let's talk about things that concern students at Yale." Is that it?

QUESTION I don't want to avoid talking about Ericka and Bobby. I *want* to talk about Ericka and Bobby. That's the point.

NEWTON Well, you can't talk about Ericka and Bobby without talking about the Vietnamese.

QUESTION But we *have* talked about the Vietnamese. We have talked about intercommunalism and the world and other countries and the future and just about everything else. But we have had practically no confrontation with things that are going on here now.

NEWTON All right, then. There's no court today, so I invite you to come to the trial on Monday. I invite you there because I refuse to talk about Bobby and Ericka here. I'll talk about them in the courtroom and outside on the Green, where our talk might mean something. But I won't indulge in your desire to merely talk in a classroom about the possibility of Bobby and Ericka going to the chair. If I feel guilty about anything, it is speaking here when they are in the docks, you see. I always feel very uncomfortable outside of the bars—when I was released from death row, I left people there—and every time I have a happy day, every time I laugh, I feel somewhat guilty.

QUESTION Well, in a sense you have said more about this whole thing in the last five seconds than you have in the whole two days before.

QUESTION The question in a lot of our minds is not that there are in existence oppressed peoples. We can see that. What is bothering us has to do with Mr. Erikson's notion of pseudospecies. Take cultural groupings like youth or blacks or Vietnamese or Chinese or North Koreans: each of them is a pseudospecies in Mr. Erikson's terms. Now one bond they all have in common is the fact that they are oppressed; they have a kind of communality for that very reason. But what happens when you attain a level where that common bond no longer exists? Will people be happy? Will no one want to become the new ruling class? I guess we have a hard time imagining some future when people no longer want to control one another.

NEWTON   We believe that the primary motivating drive of people is a will to power, a drive to free themselves from both external and internal controls. But we do not believe that this drive necessarily ends in the domination of one group of people by another: it is only because people lack knowledge and technology that their natural drive for control has been distorted into a desire for power over *people* rather than a desire for power over *things*.

So we *can* conceive of a time when people will not find it necessary to steal power from other people. Given a high level of technological knowledge, people will control the universe instead. They will make the stars go in the direction they desire, and then they can resolve their differences peacefully.

QUESTION   In that connection, do you think we can gain control of our own environment? Do you think it is too late for any of this to ever come about?

NEWTON   Too late for what to come about?

QUESTION   Well, some people speak in very pessimistic terms about the whole environment of Earth. They say it will give out in a certain number of years because our resources have been so misused.

NEWTON   They may be correct. But when we talk about the capitalists' exploitation of nature—the kind of thing discussed in what is now called the ecology movement—we often forget that people themselves are a part of the natural world. The mass murder of blacks in Africa during the slave trade, all the depredations the Europeans committed in South America and the Caribbean, the genocide committed by Nazi Europe against the Jews, the Slavs, the Gypsies, and, of course, against all people of color, are probably the greatest examples of the exploitation of nature by the capitalists. You know the greatest ecological crime being committed right now? The bombing of Vietnam. And we think that until the ecology movement starts recognizing these facts, it will remain largely irrelevant to the majority of people in the world.

People have always struggled against nature, and it is impossible for us who are struggling for the necessities of life, who have to set up our own survival programs, to talk about the struggle ending. The difference between us and the capitalists, though, is that we want a rational relationship with nature. We know that the capitalists have put us in a situation where nature cannot support us; and because we have not yet discovered the source of life, we cannot support nature either. So our struggle is twofold: we struggle to survive and gain power over our environment, and we struggle to have a rational relationship with that environment. Like I've said, we are a part of nature ourselves, so we think the difficulties we have with the environment are all in the family, you might say, and can be solved without hostility. The capitalists are not part of that family. They are madmen and will destroy nature as well as us, so our struggle to survive and gain a rational relationship with the natural world is first directed toward getting rid of these madmen.

QUESTION   Do you think that the expropriator can be expropriated soon enough for all this to happen?

NEWTON   We will do everything in our power to see that it can.

MODERATOR   I have been trying to rephrase a question in my mind which has come up over and over again this morning in one form or another. I guess everyone is ready to agree by now that one of our troubles as a species is that we have set ourselves apart into so many artificial groupings. We have been divided into nations, classes, ethnic groups; we are separated by class differences, sex lines, disparities in wealth, generation gaps, and all of that. Now you have been telling us that sooner or later these distinctions have to go and that we will have to find some way to absorb all of these individual groupings into some universal community so that we can govern the surface of the earth together. And you have a good deal of faith that the drift of human history is taking us in that direction, right? What worries me, though, is the nagging thought that if these divisions have existed so long, if mankind has always sorted itself into pseudospecies, then there must be some powerful reasons for it. This particular tendency of man started long before the capitalist era; it is as old as the species, maybe even older. But there is obviously something in the human spirit that supports it, and we had better figure out what that is before . . .

NEWTON   Now, professor, please, please. The sun has been coming up for many, many years: therefore it will come up tomorrow. Is that the way you think?

MODERATOR   I'm not saying this kind of thing is inevitable. I'm just saying it is part of the material data of human history.

NEWTON   We also know that it is negating itself. The sun might not come up tomorrow after all.

MODERATOR   Maybe, but I still worry that mankind is going to rearrange itself into other groupings as soon as the present ones disappear—unless we learn a great deal more than we know now about the process itself.

QUESTION   I wonder if this universal identity you have been talking about has anything to do with intelligence. I mean, do you think everyone can understand it? We seem to be comfortable talking about it, but I wonder how you would explain this concept to a middle American or someone in the ghetto, you know, or . . .

NEWTON   I'm from the ghetto and I understand it.

QUESTION   Yes, but you are a very intelligent person.

NEWTON   It's time for a break.

At this point, Newton got up abruptly from the table and walked over to the side of the room where refreshments had been laid out. He was visibly annoyed, and the participants around the table spoke softly but urgently to one another about what had happened. Some of it was picked up by the tape in snatches: "You know, someone could call you a racist for saying that." "But he was talking about middle Americans as well as people from the ghetto." "He didn't say that." "Look, I know what you meant, but you really implied that people from ghettoes are not intelligent."

The break lasted a good deal longer than usual, close to an hour, and the room was filled with side conversations. The transcript resumes, then, later in the morning.

MODERATOR   Professor Erikson, would you honor us with a comment?

ERIKSON   Well, you can't teach an old professor new tricks, so you invite him to honor you with a comprehensive comment. I'll try. I think we are closer to each other today. We are not altogether comfortable yet, of course, but then if we were, we would only feel like damned liars afterward. There are, for all of us, two kinds of risks involved, risks in theory and risks in commitment. What Huey and I have said so far could be discussed on a purely intellectual plane as to relevance and consistency. But the younger (and maybe some of the not so young) participants are more interested in where they stand now, more or less firmly, and where they are going if they accept our road maps. Most of the questions we have heard, therefore, seem to concern change—deliberate and enforced change. All a person like me can do is try to indicate what aspects of contemporary change he recognizes as meaningful and what he may yet hope to influence by living, acting, or maybe just writing.

But before I go on, I must say I am still smarting from that question, that nice, hospitable question, as to why in hell Huey and I came here at all. You laugh, but I think it was more hospitable to ask that question than to take it out of here unasked.

As I said, I wanted to meet Huey, especially if he wanted to meet me. And such an opportunity also fits into my main interest at present—the relativity of the individual life history and of collective history, and especially the way some individuals put their life-histories on the line, as it were, to influence the course or history. So I wanted to see how concepts like negative identity may throw light on the way in which someone like Huey Newton creates a set of new images for black and for white people. But, again, I did not come here only to hear or to make speeches. To me, the students are (and were) an essential part of the cast, even as a kind of chorus.

Now as to Huey's response to what I said about the role of explicit hate at some critical moment in a revolutionary struggle, I will concede that this has to do with certain assumptions about ritualization which may seem out of place here just because they treat theoretically what, in fact, is the most deadly issue in action. What I really meant to say is that new ritualization, like the Panthers' original action pattern, helps to bring love and hate into focus and forces a clarification where before there was ambivalence—that is, a combination of smoldering hate and cynical "law" enforcement. In this sense, I admired Huey's statement on armed love very much. This means to me— and let's see whether I really grasped it right—that we must stand ready to expect and to respond to human love in any of our fellow men so long as they do not set out to kill that human dignity in us without which we could not really love anybody. For only people with equal dignity can love each other, and this point sometimes has to be made by fighting the other—fighting him with a defined purpose and an acknowledged discipline— until he is forced to see. You see what I mean? I fight him to bring out the angel in him, so that the angel can bless both of us. So I did not mean to imply that you, Huey—and I mean you personally now—were *teaching hate*. None of your writings at the time of the founding of your Party would substantiate that. Rather, you created a confrontation which did not allow for am-

biguities and ambivalences (that is, half love and half hate) because only such a situation permits the eventual emergence of a
communality. Any other situation fosters the kind of "love"—and
God knows there is plenty of it around—which is based on reciprocal exploitation and a reciprocal cutting down of the other's
dignity. For exploitation, too, breeds exploitation. The slave, in
his symbiosis with the master, undermines the master's dignity
in many, sometimes subtle ways. The exploiter, in turn, sometimes hates the exploited to the point of wishing him dead, just
because his victim reminds him of his own absurdity. So one
must force the exploiter up against the wall of his own absurdity, as it were, before he can gain insight. Even Gandhi's nonviolent methods often seemed infuriatingly coercive to, say, the
soldiers who had to fight those unarmed and yet advancing
masses with clubs and guns. Gandhi, in fact, had deep conflicts
about the implicit aggressiveness in his massive nonaggression:
he knew very well that the masses often did not understand either armed love or unarmed militancy, because, as I said yesterday, they had not known what it means to be armed in the first
place. For that very reason, Gandhi was probably the most ex-
ultant about the time when a mountain tribe of well-trained
warriors, the Pathans, executed a perfect (and perfectly disciplined) occupation of a city which was then in the hands of a
British regiment. So much for that.

Now back to the questions about identity and pseudospecies.
Like all concepts, they are not worth more than what they help
clarify in actuality. This also assumes, I guess, that both of them
stand for processes with marked inner contradictions, such as
the positive and negative identity—the lasting tension between
which makes identity something both strong and yet vulnerable.
And it should be clear that such concepts are always both personal *and* communal. The very term "identity," of course, is apt
to sound to communalists as too individualistic and to individualists as too conformist, even though it really means to describe
processes of development which in themselves are independent

of any "isms"—although "isms" determine their conscious content. For example, whether the historical period emphasizes individualism or conformism to norms and roles and stances, the individual has to find his own identity in either. But that also means that either "ism" is, for a while, a communal integrator. If and where individualism is a dominant ideal, it can emphasize uniqueness only by way of a communal agreement which, for a while, makes individualism a life-style admired and fostered in the whole society, even if its perfection is by definition truly accessible only to an elite. Such an elite, in turn, must shoulder some responsibility for its own comportment, so as to keep the claim of uniqueness from getting out of hand and, in fact, from becoming antisocial. But then any life-style sooner or later brings forth a kind of shady "elite," which attempts to get away with something and to cover its tracks with rhetoric: before long, rhetoric makes an empty stance, a pretense, and a stereotyped role out of any liberating life-style. It makes sense, then, to speak of an eventual conspiracy between individualism and capitalism. But then I have to remind you that I am not speaking of mere ideal images or moral models, mere passing trends and fashionable styles. I am speaking of an *inner process* in every individual and in every generation involved, a process which, when things go reasonably well, guards for a while both the identities of the elite and of that majority which accepts its clues from the elite. And it is an inner process which, for a while, guards the dialectic relation of the generations and thus the sociogenetic process. I hope I do not sound too relativistic when I attempt to show the relativity of changing political and cultural styles. But there always lurks alienation and identity confusion and eventual insurrection and violence within these processes. It follows that if individualism as a cultural trend has passed its prime, then there will soon be a generation that grows up with vague ideals of individualism, that learns in college to admire the masters of a passing life-style and yet finds out before long that if you want to really "succeed" you must develop ruthless irresponsibility under the guise of pious individualistic verbiage. And if you "can't make it," you are the suckers, and you feel, to use a more noble word, "alienated." In the meantime, however, individualism in its period of flowering *has* served to establish another of those steps in human consciousness which make it ever clearer what a free man *could* be. The caricatures of decay cannot hide the true face which had been revealed, and which may well be an irreversible part of any future and more universal model of personality.

Maybe you can see now what I mean when I say that for a while a man's identity may be in line with a developing life-style, while at another time he may have to defend it, for example, by insisting on his right to be an individual in the midst of a life-style which, in fact, robs him of genuine individuality by forcing him into counterfeit individualistic roles. As you said, he may then feel that he can regain individuality only by loyally joining a communal group which stands against the prevailing life-style—or by going through a phase of inverted individualism where his inner life becomes his one and only community. (Incidentally, doesn't every writer go through such phrases, repeatedly and creatively? And if he is a novelist or dramatist, he can invent a cast representing his inner community and put it on the stage or in a novel which almost seems to have superior reality.) Today, though, all too many people can keep their inner community alive only by the use of drugs.

I have indicated, and I will repeat this here, that the identities of future men will always combine a sense of uniqueness inherited from a number of past liberations—whether religious, cultural or political—and yet also a sense of universal communality which must always again find ways of guarding itself against monopolizers and usurpers.

Well, that was quite a mouthful. But, Huey, could you accept such a psychological statement as a counterpart to your political one?

NEWTON   Yes. We say that we would like to express our

own individuality in a collective consciousness. One of our chief drives is to free the man as we bring him into the human community.

ERIKSON Then I should add that my immigration to America is now part of me—and while I would not want to overlook the possibility that we may see things differently as a result, I also feel strongly that without that development called the United States of America and, yes, even the technological imperialism that we deplore so much when it oversteps the limits of human comprehension and compassion—that without it we would not sit here talking as we do. That means that we have a common faith (maybe only because one must have a faith in survival) that each pseudospecies and each empire in some dialectical way added new elements to a more universal sense of humanity.

NEWTON Yes, and I would take that further and say that without imperialism there would be no reactionary intercommunalism, and without reactionary intercommunalism there would be no revolutionary intercommunalism; and so it follows that imperialism lays a foundation for world communism. It is necessary for imperialism to exist, even though we don't like it: that's the internal contradiction, you see. I would agree with that. I'm not happy about it, but that is the dialectics of the situation.

ERIKSON I came across that form of dialectics fifteen years ago when I wrote about young Martin Luther's identity crisis within the historical crisis of the Catholic empire. Incidentally, I heard recently that some young priests in Rome are reading the Italian translation of my Luther book now—enough to make the Pope publicly scoff at their claim of undergoing an identity crisis. But you cannot start an ecumenical movement without arousing identity conflicts and historical doubts which make these young priests hear the echo of that long-forbidden German voice; or, more probably, ecumenicism would not emerge without the prior existence of such conflicts and doubts.

All of this is on the way to overcoming such pseudospeciation as the Church of Rome, too, has indulged in.

Now I might mention that I recently reported, in a meeting where representatives of other fields did the same, on the possible connection between my particular life in these particular times and the fact that I was the person who first described and named the "identity crisis," a concept which immediately took. I think it is important to be aware of the reasons why some ideas prove importable and exportable. For example, I think that psychoanalysis was welcome in this country more than anywhere else because it promised to the self-made man a tool to remake in himself what he had brought along by dint of his origins. Psychoanalysis, for some, replaced lost orthodoxies. At the same time, in a country to which the management of things and people was the highest endeavor, psychoanalysis seemed to promise more efficient self-management and, in fact, the management of sexuality, aggression, and even love. The mechanistic terms used in psychoanalysis, for reasons going back into the scientific climate of the turn of the century, acquired an even more metallic sound here—terms like "defense mechanism" and "transference," for example. And the prominent use of the ancient term "ego" no doubt appealed to a wide consumership because people took it by its American meaning. In this way, ideas emerge from and come to serve the material culture.

QUESTION   Mr. Erikson, yesterday you closed your talk with a quote from Marx—something to the effect that until there is a revolution no one can really become an adult. Now I would imagine that Marx was talking about the fact that various impingements of class and race and sex and so on prevent one from moving into real adulthood. They are part of his identity and affect him in ways he is not conscious of. Marx obviously thought that once a revolution takes place and wealth is redistributed, then these changes in the material world would result in similar changes in the psychological world. But how do an individual's inner perceptions get influenced by his material surroundings? To what extent are basic human drives derived *from* material conditions and to what extent are they changed *by* material conditions? I guess I am really asking how the material dialectic and the psychological dialectic relate to one another.

ERIKSON   A good question. Yes, indeed, if I could only answer *that* one. All I can say right now is that the dialectics of the generational process mediates between the material and the psychological. This, at least, would give us some access to your question. But as to my quoting Marx, I only meant to indicate that he may have had something in mind analogous to this pseudospecies business. To him, the various levels of technology bring about a division of labor and a division of standardized roles which assigns to each individual a specific place in a system of production and exploitation. This makes him unfree in that it robs him of those of his potentials which are not immediately useful or which may even be inimical to the defined role he must accept. Alienated from his own inner nature and alienated from nature, he cannot be said to be a true adult. In psychological terms, one could say that his identity is overdetermined by his assigned circumstances, and that what he must suppress in himself becomes partially projected on others, so that he can neither permit others nor himself to be "wholly human." In other words—well, would you say Lincoln was a reasonably adult man?

NEWTON   No.

ERIKSON   Next question! Well, let me quote anyway what came to my mind. Lincoln said: "As I would not be slave, I would not be master." That seems to me a rather adult statement—for his time, of course.

NEWTON   I read his other letters. But go on.

ERIKSON   I call this statement relatively adult because it is a beautifully parsimonious expression of a man's insight into his total situation at a certain moment of history. It includes, in my terms, the assumption that you cannot be fully yourself if your identity depends on somebody else's identity loss, a potentially vicious symbiosis in the sense that each lives—and dies—off the other. This is a parallel to what Huey said about the reciprocity of the dignity of love. But to get at the dynamics of this, psychoanalysis will have to go beyond adapting individuals to the status quo, or, for that matter, consider adulthood a mere matter of leaving one's childhood behind. It will have to provide the conceptual means for an adult to recognize his status (or is it flux) in historical change, and his responsibility toward the next generation. Does that answer you?

QUESTION   I guess it answers about two-thirds of it.

ERIKSON   Two-thirds! Either I am doing well or you are being too polite.

QUESTION   You know, most students seem to have this thing about following someone or something and not really becoming concerned themselves. And it seems to me that just your mere presence here, Mr. Newton, forces me to some kind of subjective analysis: there are certain things that I am going to have to do sooner or later, certain conclusions that I am going to have to reach for myself about this society and whether I want to fit into it or try to effect some type of change. It seems to me that everyone is sort of running away from themselves right now. I mean, it is easier to take what you were saying and try to attack it than it is to look inward and try to reach something inside; and that's what seems to have been happening for the past two days. People are saying, "Well, Huey, what do you think about this?" and "Well, Huey, you are wrong about that"; and, you know, I can challenge you from ten different stances at once without ever having to face the basic questions you are raising within myself. As far as I am concerned, though, this whole discussion is about alternatives—and I think your mere presence here is an alternative. I don't know.

QUESTION   I would like to comment on that too, because it seems to me that Mr. Newton is very, very committed to what he has been talking about and most of us just don't know how to be. He says that he's not an idealist, but at the same time he is willing to sacrifice his life for what he believes in. And, let's face it, a lot of people do not want to commit themselves that far because they . . .

NEWTON They'll commit themselves. Uncle Sam calls and they will be over on the soil of the Vietnamese people risking their lives and even giving up their lives. It's not a question of giving up your life. The real question is: For what cause will you give up your life?

We in the Black Panther Party will not give up our lives when the ruling circles call for us to do so. We would rather give up our lives trying to expropriate the ruling circles. Now I don't like having to make that choice, because I would rather see all of humanity resolving its contradictions by discussions like this. But it is idealistic to think we can do so now: the simple fact that people must fight to end division shows a low development at this time for all of mankind.

QUESTION You have said several times that the Panther Party is mainly involved in an educational program. But I guess I don't really understand exactly *what* you do to relate to people on the human level, how you set yourselves up as examples of the kind of thing you are talking about. I mean, what do you actually *do*?

NEWTON Well, we have what we call a ten-point program. It's called a survival program—survival until the people become more self-conscious and mature, because until then we are all in danger of genocide. Members of the Party spend most of their time setting up these programs and helping run them.

These programs are open to everyone in the community. We have health clinics; we have a busing program for parents and relatives and friends of prisoners who would not be able to visit the prison otherwise because they do not have the money; and we have clothing programs, especially on the East Coast because of the winter cold. Now these are reformist kinds of programs, but they have been integrated into the rest of our revolutionary program. We do them all over the country and we are expanding them. We know they won't solve the problem. But because we are interested in the people, we serve the people.

QUESTION   The question was raised several times yesterday and again today about whether the Panthers have been operating over the past few years more by political intuition or more by the ideology which has been described here. I suppose the answer to that has to be that you need both in order to get off the ground: you need political intuition, obviously, to get some sense of how to proceed, and, once started, you need an ideology to enable people to understand what you are doing.

NEWTON   Political science, not intuition. We have always had an ideology and have always attempted to practice our theory. We studied the situation from the very start; we had a program from the very start.

QUESTION   All right. But the ideology as you have spelled it out seems to me less relevant once you leave the stage where victims are actively resisting oppression and enter the stage of universal consciousness. Do you see what I mean? I am not sure that your ideology is nearly as useful in offering a blueprint for arriving at that future stage as it has been for getting out of the stage we are in. It seems to me this is what people mean when they keep asking you: Where do we go from here? The usefulness of your ideology is that it mobilizes an enormous amount of human energy against a rather rigid structure and a rather fixed set of situations. But we are not going to need that so much anymore, because . . .

NEWTON   The Vietnamese don't need it?

QUESTION   Now wait a minute. I'm talking about the future, the way the future is going to emerge. We have set up a system, a technological system, which rests on science and which determines the kinds of interconnectedness that we will have to deal with. In the long run, we are going to have to manage an enormously complicated plant. And this creates a different situation from the one in which we have lived as men for five thousand years. We are all involved with a large, complex technical system which we have got to manage somehow or it will get out of control. And I guess what I miss in your ideology is some way of defining the new institutions, the new ideas, that will enable us to control that evolution. So my first question is: How are we going to manage the plant? Have you been thinking about that?

NEWTON   Oh, yes. We are definitely thinking about it.

QUESTION   And then my second question is for Mr. Erikson. If we evolve into a kind of interconnectedness where people have to give up some of their separate interests, their sense of difference, aren't we going to need a new kind of person? We are going to have to give up some of ourselves in order to reach accommodation, it seems to me, and this will involve us in some kind of struggle to maintain our identity while reconciling our differences with others. Or, to put it another way, how can we retain shreds of identity in a rapidly changing system when we are constantly asked to accommodate to others at the same time we are managing that huge plant?

ERIKSON   Well, I am not sure I entirely understand what you mean. Where our identity is in shreds, there is a bad situation however you look at it. Yet, as you indicate, it might be necessary for us to realize the impossibility of ever achieving an identity as fully formed, as static, as secure, as could be done (or so it now seems) in past periods. This, in fact, is probably the reason why we, in our time, have begun to become so self-conscious about identity processes. There could even be a kind of evolutionary adaptation in such clinical awareness, for perceptive clinicians may learn to recognize in the dominant neurotic disturbances of the age a shift in psychosocial processes. This adds awareness (at first often painful and anxiety provoking) to the dominant conflicts of an age, and I think you stated well some of the sacrifices of a secure and even superior sense of identity which we have to allow in order to give more people a chance to have some kind of identity at all. But that does not

mean that our identities are in shreds, not yet; for identity formation can adapt itself to multiple demands. While it is true
that some basic design is formed in adolescence, such a design
need not—and should not—foreclose all variations for once and
for all. Identity development, while given a decisive direction in
adolescence, never really ends; and it is quite possible in principle that rapid changes in technology and culture can count on
some adaptiveness of identity throughout life—that is, if appro-
priate social forms are invented which create leeway through
new forms of association and cooperation. And here, you see,
what so many of us deplore—the open-endedness of the American identity—may, in fact, be a great contribution to a more universal identity fit for a world-wide technology. For that very
reason, American identity must now undergo a crisis, for, in becoming universal, it must also realize its historical limitations.
Unlimited possibilities, as we now know, can land you in unfore-
seen dead ends—real *dead ends.* This is really hard for the
American people to accept; it undermines the whole ethos of
work and success. It feels, in fact, like a defeat, and the self-mis-
made man becomes sulky and angry. If we only had leaders
who could convince our people that to have the insight and the
guts to recognize the limitations of one's destiny, now *that*
would be victory!

One other question should be discussed in this context, too:
What is going to happen to those masses—and they are not only
to be found in middle America—whose identity is vitally related
to the running of industries? It's interesting, isn't it, how little
those of us who work on the border between humanist and revolutionary imageries think of the vast mass of people who have
become the human tools of industrialization as well as the con-
sumers of what is produced by it. How would a general dénoue-
ment of the American technological know-how affect them, and
what alternative identifications are available in this stage of
technology? Will they indulge, by necessity, in new forms of reactionary intercommunalism? And doesn't Huey speak primarily

for another part of the population of the world—those who are moving from a tradition of ex-colonial agrarianism into a kind of anarchic urbanization? I would, in fact, claim that many radical intellectuals, because of their preoccupation with traditional literary models, are nostalgically hung up on such identity conflicts and prefer to ignore the real conflicts of the modern working man.

It's getting late, and I would like to come back to at least one of the many questions which I could not answer earlier. Yes, pseudospeciation, no matter how it started, has become a powerful need for the human race, having absorbed not only specifically human habits of imagination but also instinctive forces working for orientation and adaptation. This combination has, in fact, led to a paradox which can only be called man's *pseudologia realis*, that is, his tendency to wrap solid facts and effective techniques into visionary world images to make-believe and usurpation. I can only suggest that we study this carefully, for it seems that neither moral outrage nor fresh utopian commitments can change this trend to ever new illusions, leading eventually to the same old power struggles. Without new insights, we must really fear new outbreaks of that reactionary pseudospeciation which found (we hope) its climax in Hitler, and we may well wonder what will become of some of our era's liberations when the liberated will face each other as brothers, each a god on earth.

The conversation continued for a few moments in an effort to pick up old threads, but the New Haven meetings were clearly over.

PART II

Meetings in Oakland

IN THE MONTH that followed the meetings in New Haven, it happened that four persons who had been heavily involved in the earlier gathering met in various groupings to talk about it. Erik Erikson spent the month of March in the San Francisco Bay area and met several times with Huey Newton. Herman Blake and Kai Erikson, the one a black sociologist from the University of California at Santa Cruz and the other a white sociologist from Yale, met twice in New Haven to compare notes. And, to complete the cycle, Blake and the older Erikson also spent some time together in Oakland. So it seemed logical and perhaps even inevitable that the four of us would pick up the hanging threads and continue. At the end of March, then, we gathered in Newton's Oakland apartment and the second round of talks began.

As the following transcript makes clear, the tone of the second meeting was distinctly different from the first. In the first place, the participants were by now better acquainted and more comfortable in one another's company. In the second place, the formality which had been imposed upon us in New Haven by the need for security and the sheer weight of numbers was no longer a factor. And in the third place, we had a natural subject with which to begin—a review of what had happened at Yale.

A good deal has been written in the press about Newton's apartment: that it is elegant and expensive, that it sits high above the streets of Oakland and thus commands a sweeping view of the bay, that it has wall-to-wall carpeting, sliding glass partitions, and a number of other luxuries. All of that is true. What is not said in the press, however, is that the apartment is almost as spare as a cell. The walls are bare of decorations, the furniture impersonal, and the apartment itself sits twenty-five floors above the streets where Huey Newton grew up and lived most of his years—twenty-five floors above the smell of honest cooking and the sound of everyday life and the flow of real human activity. Both literally and figuratively, this is a high price to pay for security, and most of the people who have felt disappointed or irritated because a revolutionary leader lives in such expensive circumstances have not really given very much thought to what they mean.

The living room of the suite is dominated by a large television set: during the time I was there it was tuned to a closed-circuit channel and focused on the front door so that a viewer could monitor the traffic coming in or going out. In the bedroom there is a superb telescope, a present to Huey on the occasion of his thirtieth birthday. When I saw it, it was attached to a tripod and trained at a small window across Lake Merritt. In the glare of the California sun, one cannot see anything in that window; but in the evening, apparently, one can make out the faint silhouettes of people as they pass back and forth behind the opening. Newton spends hours observing that scene. It is the little death row of the county jail.

Discussions with *J. HERMAN BLAKE,* *ERIK H. ERIKSON, KAI T. ERIKSON,* and *HUEY P. NEWTON*

Oakland, California, March 31, 1971

KTE   We were talking about the meetings in New Haven...

HPN   My preconception about the meeting was that I would be at odds with you, Erik, as a psychoanalyst. I didn't know that you had developed a new approach to the understanding of man's behavior. After I read a number of the essays and books you had written, I was impressed; your approach took the edge off of what I thought would be my attack, you see, because I was ready to view it as an adversary kind of thing. Then after starting the seminar at Yale, I was somewhat on the defensive because of the general environment. There were a number of people there who were more likely than not to misunderstand. And I was more likely than not to misunderstand, too, because in a setting like that you tend to want to answer as quickly as possible, to come out looking and feeling all right about it. In that kind of environment, one might miss the purpose of the whole thing.

EHE   I suggested to Kai that whatever title we agree on,

the word "search" or "exploration" should be in it. We were really in an exploratory mood in New Haven, and that was the meaning of the whole thing. But, of course, I was on the defensive too—wondering from which direction your offensive was going to come, and feeling that we were an odd pair of contestants. We are obviously an old man and a young man, an immigrant to America and a black man coming out of that American reality which I did not know and, no doubt, preferred not to know at first. And then, too, I am a psychoanalyst at the end of his career, a certified professor, already emeritus; and you are a young man who has put his life and liberty on the line in the service of a future as yet unclear to me. So on every score we were apt to talk *by* each other at first—which is actually what happened at the scheduled meetings, even though we were relating privately in ways I was not yet willing to share in public. When you come right down to it, I am the kind of person who has to *respond* to what is going on in the world with psychoanalytic insight, which I realize now you can accept up to a point. But I could not be sure when we first met that you would not feel like calling me some kind of names—because, you see, I thrived on that system that exploited your people, thrived in spite of being an immigrant, a former dropout, and (then no general recommendation) a Freudian. And then, just before we met, I had received a certain amount of publicity—my picture on the cover of magazines and all that—because a book about me had just come out. I felt particularly vulnerable then. My book on Gandhi is the closest I have come in understanding revolutionary action.

JHB What was the role of the students in the conference? What were they looking for? What were they expecting?

KTE I don't know. As I look back on the whole affair, I sometimes worry that I handled it poorly. It all began with a phone call from Don Freed, as I guess you know, and our thinking at the time was that it would be nice for you, Huey, and later for you, Pop, to compare ideas with one another in a room full of thoughtful students. I suppose I actually had two things in mind. For one, I am a teacher and I just wanted students to hear and share in the discussions. And then, frankly, I also wanted to avoid bringing a lot of other professionals into the conference who have their own particular lines of thought to offer—Yale is full of them, of course—because I thought our agenda would get so crowded. It seemed to me that "intercommunalism" and "the wider identity" were about as much as we could handle in a three-day workshop, and I did not want other people hawking their own wares. I didn't even hawk my own (to the great irritation of my esteemed colleague here) and maybe I was just too sensitive on that score. It might have been interesting to hear what people like Bob Lifton or Bill Coffin or Ken Keniston would have made of the proceedings.

EHE   In retrospect, would you have liked to have some of those people there?

HPN   I think it would have been interesting. I didn't think the students made the contribution they could have.

KTE   Well, one problem was that the conference got out of hand in terms of scale. If I had to do it over, I wouldn't locate the whole thing in that enormous library: it's Ivy League to the core. And there were simply too many people in the room. Several of the students I talked to felt they were in some kind of theater, acting out a script they hadn't seen yet.

JHB   Perhaps. But it seemed to me that the students were reflecting a general public attitude—an image of Huey Newton and the Black Panther Party which is uninformed and unenlightened—and I frankly doubt that they saw the conference as an opportunity to become exposed to new ideas. I thought some of the students were surprised to see Huey without his shotgun. I would be interested in knowing from you, Erik, what your first reaction was to Huey's articulation of revolutionary intercommunalism. Is this the direction you expected him to come from? The reason I ask is that I have a concern which is shared by many persons who have become revolutionary. People who sit in positions of power and influence keep saying, "We're doing all right, what's the matter with you that you can't fit in?" They cannot seem to accept as legitimate the fact that someone has done an objective and serious analysis of the system they live in and has consciously made the decision not to be a part of it. For people like that, to even give serious thought to the ideas of the Party is to question their lives, their selves, their beings, their positions; and so they spend all their time trying to rationalize the matter, to push the Party back into the system or even to psychoanalyze it out of existence. I'm wondering to what extent those kinds of sentiments were coming through.

EHE   Well, as to that last point, I probably should have stressed earlier that the very fact of my being a psychoanalyst makes me hold back with criticism or critique. I've seen psychoanalytical explanations used as weapons—either of offense or defense—only too often, and I have tried to learn not to do that. I want to first understand the whole situation and then see where any psychoanalytic explanations might fit in. So I guess I held back exactly in that area where, from your previous experience, you thought I might let go.

JHB   Yes.

EHE   No wonder the students felt that neither of us really let go. They felt, I would imagine—and, Kai, you correct me if I am wrong—they felt that you, Huey, were so theoretical that they could barely recognize the man with the gun and wondered if you were holding back for reasons of academic environment. At the same time, they half-expected that I would light into you, asking about your background, your personality, in an effort to figure out the unconscious determinants of your revolutionary leanings—which, come to think of it, is what I did do in the case of Luther and Gandhi, but only after long study of their voluminous confessional utterances. So maybe the students felt a little betrayed: they came to a spectacle in which Huey was going to be aggressive and I was going to be psychoanalytic and the sparks would fly.

KTE   And that is certainly how we arranged the room: like a Roman spectacle.

EHE   They felt each of us betrayed our mandate, in a way, and that we overadjusted to those rows of books all around us.

KTE   I think that is partly so, but something else may have been going on at the same time. Most of the students I know want to relate more closely to people they admire or are interested in. They wanted to hear a little more from each of you about who you are, what you are thinking, and how all of that is connected to the realities of their lives. But what they got was theory—and a pretty abstract brand of theory at that. They wanted to be responded to, accepted as deserving people, and I am not sure that they were.

EHE   I could make that clear to myself in terms of my own theory and say that first of all they wanted to identify and then they wanted to understand. So they were mostly interested in challenging Huey—in finding out how they might identify with or against him and what he could mean to their identity choices.

KTE   That's it. They were more interested in coming to terms with Huey as a person than with intercommunalism as an idea, which certainly isn't hard to understand.

EHE   And that's their birthright, of course. We should remember, too, that one of their dominant conflicts right now is between being students in order to study for an occupation and a profession and a career, or being students so as to be informed activists in the meantime. I don't know what is going on at Yale right now, but when I came out here a month ago a number of professors at the University of California told me how depressed the students are because they don't see at this moment any genuine access to activism; and I'm not sure that we didn't get some of that conflict at Yale. You know what I mean?

HPN   Sort of . . .

EHE   And when you, of all people, talked like a damned professor!

HPN   Well, they're not the only ones I have had *that* problem with.

JHB   But I wonder if that didn't paralyze them a bit.

KTE   It's funny. You know, a lot of people were upset because they thought we had chosen nothing but conservative students for the conference—and maybe they were in some abstract class sense—but in the Yale scheme of things a number of them were reckoned to be rather radical.

JHB   Well, we won't go into that.

KTE   How about radical with a small *r*?

JHB   No, I know what you mean. I think one of the things people don't understand or refuse to see is that the Black Panther Party is not just some willy-nilly helter-skelter bunch of people who run around trying to upset everybody. It is a program, a distinct pattern of thinking and ideology, delivering certain conclusions from which strategies and actions derive. The ideology is critical here; revolutionary intercommunalism is a way of visualizing reality so that people can understand the critique the Panthers have been developing all along. It's not simply that Huey talks like a professor, which I wouldn't deny for a moment, but that people cannot accept the logic of what he says because they are not ready to go that far.

KTE   I suppose that's true too. But students have not really heard very much ideology before. Radical politics on campus has largely been a thing of action, movement, feeling, protest; students are just not accustomed to hearing anyone present a calm and reasoned ideological statement, no matter how revolutionary its thrust. That's one reason why the young white radicals these days and the older socialist radicals who learned their politics in the thirties and forties have such a hard time getting together. Have you heard very many serious ideological conversations on campus?

JHB   No, I haven't. I agree with you. A lot of students just do this and do that without thought, although it's understandable when you consider that they spend so much time in classrooms (I just thought I'd toss that in). But in my opinion, and in the opinion of some of the colleagues with whom I work very closely, revolutionary activity without serious planning and thought is in fact counterrevolutionary.

HPN As a matter of fact, that's a very good statement about unplanned action—about revolutionary action and counterrevolutionary action. Young people generally feel that the role of the revolutionary is to define a set of actions and a set of principles that are easy to identify and are absolute. But what I was trying to explain to them was the *process*: revolution, basically, is a contradiction between the old and the new in the process of development. Anything can be revolutionary at a particular point in time, but most of the students don't understand that. And most other people don't understand it either.

JHB What was your reaction, Erik, to Huey's original statement? I've always wondered about that.

EHE I've wondered too. Much of it I simply didn't understand, to tell you the truth—or maybe I was just waiting for a combined personal and intellectual impression without which I do not "understand." Maybe what we just said should have been the very introduction to the whole thing, the relation of revolutionary action to revolutionary ideology and theory. I am glad that our readers—if it comes to that—will have a chance to hear this, because otherwise some might have the same difficulty we attributed to the students of not appreciating that there are a number of different passions in a revolutionary. Hot action is one of them, cold theory is another; and we have been exploring the affinities of the two in political and psychological theory. Incidentally, if I may change the subject slightly, it seems to me now that it was a mistake for me to *begin* my remarks in New Haven by comparing the young Newton and the older Newton. I meant that half humorously, of course. I did not mean to say that these are two different Hueys, but I wanted to remind the students that you are the same man who is always pictured with the gun. Maybe I should have said then exactly what I said just now about the several passions that a revolutionary has; that all revolutionaries, even when armed, love to argue things in theoretical and ideological terms. Didn't you come to the meetings with the expectation that that was understood?

HPN   Not really. That's why I said in the beginning that we were dropouts and that the students would need more of an explanation because they wouldn't understand. Dropouts understand things students don't.

JHB   Erik, would you be a little more specific about what you expected?

EHE   Oh, no, we have talked enough about that. I just did not expect to hear a sermon on materialism as a theory. But why not? I was glad to listen. I should repeat, however, that I did expect others to participate more: we had two sociologists and a historian there, after all, not to mention the students coming from how many different academic fields, and I definitely felt that there should have been a number of other approaches represented there to help fill in the spaces between the ideological and the psychological. I listened for where my concepts might fit in, and that's what I responded to on the second day. In the background, of course, there were always two great spirits, Marx and Freud. If we have any theoretical grandfathers in common, they are Marx and Freud—and maybe Darwin as well, but that's something else again. In historical perspective, the young Marx and the young Freud were much less far apart from each other than was the case when they became Marx and Freud. So if we could not resolve the relationship of materialism and psychology, we went on living that historical split. You must remember that where materialism entered psychology, it became behaviorism, which is not my field, and I think that one of the names I expected to be called was "idealist." So where does that leave us? Can one be a materialist psychologist without reducing everything to conditioned reflexes?

HPN   I would only consider a psychologist or a psychoanalyst an idealist if he attempted to explain the phenomenon of personality strictly in nonmaterial terms—in other words, if he did not acknowledge that the "spiritual" side of a person finds its genesis in a material source, you see. You would agree with that, wouldn't you?

EHE Sure, I would agree with that.

Now some of your materialist friends or readers, of course, might think that you shouldn't have a conversation with me or anyone else coming from the Freudian establishment. But, on the other hand, I feel that I, in my time, also, have been part of a kind of "revolution"—even though we might want to put the word in quotation marks. Now I believe that a revolutionary of the future would at least implicitly have to acknowledge some of what we have found out about man's nature or he would be in danger of rerepressing it to the disadvantage of the kind of forward vision which is part of any true "movement." In the lives and struggles of revolutionaries, all kinds of unconscious motivations are obvious which, they must sooner or later recognize, have little to do with their professed rationales. In understanding such unconscious motivations, maybe one could avoid such destructive developments as where old comrades fight each other as mortal enemies. But maybe this is just a necessary part of the history of all revolutions—all *past* ones, at any rate.

HPN I remember we talked in New Haven about the necessity for contradictions, the reality of contradictions, in everything. It is the same with the social as it is with the physical and biological world. Old things clash and then new things emerge, showing characteristics of both the old and the new.

EHE Herman or Kai, would you want to say something about what I have said so far? How about psychoanalysis as a method, for example: can you accept it as enlightening?

JHB Well, I can certainly accept it as enlightening, but I think the problem is that it is so often used as a tool to help people adjust to their circumstances when it is time to help them recognize that it is the circumstances, not the people, that are aberrant. A lot of what passes for illness, it seems to me, are the rational reactions of rational people to irrational conditions. A good part of sociological theory has the same basis—an implicit assumption that this is the best of all possible worlds, and that even though it may not be as good as it ought to be, somehow or other we have to adjust to it as it is. That is an unacceptable position to me.

KTE I'd agree with that.

EHE You know, what all of this leads to is the question of what is reality. Maybe materialism offers a simple solution to the problem of defining reality: in psychoanalysis and sociology, though, "reality" is often little more than those circumstances which a given elite can make appear real because they dominate the media of communication.

JHB I would like to take another approach and define reality as the substance of the experiences of a group of people, even though they may not call it that. In many black communities, for example, the experiences of the people are often summarized in a religious kind of panegyric, right? Now I am not ready to go so far as to say that these kinds of religious convictions and commitments and expectations constitute reality, but I am willing to recognize that this is a way of coping with a kind of reality which has been seen as uncopable before. The Black Panther Party put its office in West Oakland between two locales that are very familiar to the population there. One of them is the Mt. Zion Spiritual Temple, featuring a kind of folk catholicism, and the other is a dance hall called the Continental Club. These places have always represented two methods of escape from that reality. Now the Party is trying to deal with that reality in another manner. . . . A colleague of mine, Leroy Bennett, once made a beautiful statement to the effect that what is ignored in historical research is the fact that George Washington and George Washington's slaves lived two different realities. People seem to think that because they live in the same geographical space and in the same period they must be living the same reality, but there are several realities and the official one is defined by power.

EHE   O.K. That is what I meant. . . . Now I wonder if I could turn to another topic entirely and ask you, Huey, to talk a little about the principle of inner contradiction. That is something that most people, including the students at Yale, do not get and are apparently not prepared to get. Where and how do we both use it? For example, I would say that a positive and a negative identity are a dialectical given in each person. But let's come to that later and see what contradiction means in your sense and how it could be clarified for people like the students. What has your kind of contradiction to do not only with the dialectical but also with relativity and complementarity? All this is hard for students. It's hard for everyone, really, but we have let the students stand for so many things in our conversations that they might as well represent "everyone" for the moment.

HPN   I don't think the students are taught dialectically, and one of the reasons they are not is that it would be detrimental to the bourgeois educational system to do so. I think it is a fair statement that the schools are agencies of the status quo: the bourgeoisie needs to train technicians and to give students a conglomeration of facts, but it would be detrimental for them to give students the tools to show that the status quo cannot stand and so to analyze them out of existence. So I think it is more than just a question of students "having a hard time."

EHE   I even have a feeling that some of them did not understand what you meant by "idealism." They weren't sure whether you were talking about *ideas* or *ideals*. So when you spoke of contradictions, my feeling was that some thought it was something one must avoid, not something that is intrinsically necessary. It is very difficult for students to be asked to believe that we all are living contradictions—and cannot help it.

KTE   One difficulty here, it seems to me, is that Huey uses dialectics to deal with the emerging present, to discuss things that are in the process of becoming. Students and professors, on the other hand, more often use dialectical reasoning to explain what happened in the past—why Hannibal acted as he did, and so on. A lot of academics assume without really saying so that

one is free from a dialectical process the moment one under-
stands it, you see what I mean? So Huey comes and tells everyone that they are a part of the very process they are talking
about whether they want to be or not. That's pretty scary at
twenty, you know. It's scary at forty. Now you may be comfortable seeing your own views as transitory or the truth as
you see it now as temporary, but most people are not. Not in the
universities, anyway.

HPN   I don't know how comfortable I am, either.

EHE   We can't afford to forget how young these students
are—which is why I reminded us all of the fantastic things you
did, Huey, when you were in your early twenties. The students
are looking—you know I even have a term for it, I call it "total-
ism"—they are looking for totalistic explanations and not for relativistic analysis. A total explanation is something you can
totally identify with or against, a stable point of reference
against which you can know where you are.

JHB   Yeah, but why do you think they are doing that, Erik?

EHE   I think they are doing it because that is part of being
young—and I agree entirely with you that this is also what
opens them up for a kind of complete indoctrination by some
system. Some of them are quite willing to remain open, of
course, but that is a scary state to be in.

HPN   The main thing I am saying is that they don't know
how to go about it. And the reason they don't know how is because it is convenient for the schools not to teach them that. It's
better to give them a conglomeration of facts to remember so
that they can be used by whatever employer or profession they
go into, and never step outside of it.

EHE   Maybe all of this has something to do with what you
are trying to do in your course, Herman, when you speak of the
complementarity (that's the word I would use, at any rate) of
emotion and thought. You want the students to feel, right? But
then you complain because you get so many papers in return

that are emotional but not thoughtful. While what you really want to teach them is to feel and then to be able to stand back and think about what they felt.

JHB Right.

EHE And then to step back and see what kinds of feeling were in that thought. Isn't that what you had in mind?

JHB That's the way I'm approaching that class, yes.

EHE That is the way you are approaching that class, but you must notice how hard it is for that age to do what you ask.

JHB Yes. But I still think there is a more fundamental problem here. There are all these self-serving theories which seem to suggest that you reach a point where process stops, where transformation ends.

HPN That's what happens when you get into power.

JHB That's right, that's right. And what I am trying to say is that students see themselves as in process, in transition from childhood to adulthood; but they always want to know where the process stops. You see what I mean?

EHE It is exactly at this point where my ideas about identity are easily misunderstood as meaning that once you become identical with a role, then the process stops and you know where you are. That is why the most common way identity is represented is as an answer to the question "Who am I?"—a definition of identity I have never used and never would use, because the answer to the question "Who am I?" (if there really were one) would end the process of becoming itself. Real identity formation, of course, is a continuous process with a special crisis in youth—and, I would think, it is a dialectical process, which is what we may yet want to talk about.

KTE Well, how about it, Huey? Does the dialectical process ever end?

HPN I think that after the dialectical process has run its course, man will reach a state of godliness—and that's because I think God is mostly what man has said "I am not." Now that's just long-range speculation, of course. We'll have to live with dialectics for a while yet.

EHE   Now about positive and negative identities? If you assume everybody has a set of self-images which he has learned he should strive for and a set of images he has learned he should avoid—and yet he is always both, because real identity cannot be anything but an interplay of these things. Now, would you call that dialectics?

HPN   Yes, I think that is a beautiful example.

EHE   You see, some students seem to hope that by studying my stuff they will learn what a positive identity is and how to get rid of the negative one. Another group of students is afraid of my stuff because they think what I mean by identity is to be so adjusted to the system that you don't want to be anything else but what the system permits you to be. And neither of these explanations represent what I meant. The trouble starts when you project your own negative identity on other people.

JHB   We have talked a lot about the meetings at Yale. I would like to change directions for a moment and go back to a matter that Erik has always been interested in: maybe it's time to talk about the gun.

EHE   Well, actually, that fits right in here. You see, when I started to talk in New Haven I reminded the students of the traditional image which Huey used to represent and which still appears on the cover of the Panther paper—the young black man with the gun. All of this became more dialectical in our conversations when you, Huey, began to speak about arms and love. I thought I understood what you meant to some extent because of something that became clear to Gandhi as he developed his nonviolent method—namely, that most people seem to feel that to be nonviolent means not to *have* any gun and not to *want* any gun because one would not want to use it or would not know how to use it anyway. But there is an intermediary step between violence and nonviolence where you have a gun but use it only in the most disciplined way—in part, at least, to show up the absurdity of particular kinds of armed violence. This, I think, you did on several important occasions which really created your original public image. I hope you see now what I mean. You were not afraid to carry that gun. Now I would understand armed love to mean that one can really love only if one knows that one could and would defend one's dignity, for only two people of equal dignity can love each other. There is no use trying to love somebody who denies you dignity or to whom you deny it. In this sense, then, there is a dialectical relation between violence and nonviolence, and the last thing I would want to imply here is that your earlier image is inconsistent with the things you are saying and doing now. Both together make up a historical step and (I would assume) a very personal step, and you needed the one for the other. I don't know whether you would agree to that. You would now accept the gun-carrying image, wouldn't you, as historically necessary and valid?

HPN   I think it served a strategic purpose—although I imagine historians are going to make a lot out of it.

EHE   You mean like I just did?

HPN   No, no. It's just that so much has been written about the whole business of the armed self-defense of the community, and I haven't seen one thing that's accurate. I'm not talking about you, Erik; I think your interpretation is fair. But I just sort of shiver whenever I see books written on the matter.

EHE   For example, Bobby Seale describes some of the things you two did in the early days of the Party that, to me, seemed to amount to a parallel with the Gandhi technique—although I assume you didn't know about it then or, at any rate, it was not uppermost in your mind. When you faced down those policemen, for example—not threatening them with your guns or indicating with gestures that you would shoot first, but daring them to shoot first. That was a very important psychological condition you created there. You gave them the initiative and said, "O.K., you shoot first." All of this is probably related somehow to the old western frontier scenario, where the cowboys used to make this kind of confrontation a supreme test as to who would be quicker on the trigger. But you made something very different and, in a way, very revolutionary out of it when you made it clear that you didn't come to shoot them, but if they had come to shoot you, then they should come out with it. You paralyzed them morally, don't you think?

HPN   Well, I would agree that they were paralyzed at least.

KTE   But why were they paralyzed?

HPN   They had never been required to cope with a situation like that one. Because of their own racism, their own misconception of the black community and the black psyche, they did not know how to deal with the fact that we were not afraid of them, you see? And they were very provocative.

EHE   This kind of transvaluation can be a historical act, and Bobby Seale has a very good sense of how to describe such things—with humor, too. For example, how you would stand there with a few of your men and would confront those policemen and all the armed power they had behind them. Now, of course, you shouldn't be surprised if they afterward should feel endangered in their essence. It has often been said about Gandhi that he could only have done what he did with the British and not anyone else. All of that fits rather well into what you refer to as the dialectical development of empires. You see, Gandhi met the British head-on with their own ideas of fairness, ideas they had widely established as an ideal, and when he faced them down with that they simply had to accept it as a lesson. It could well be that a policeman whose background does not include any kind of experience with this kind of thing would simply say to himself—"Okay, to hell with it, I'll get him some other time." What I learned in studying Gandhi was how he could give to a concrete object—and this is what I meant to apply to the gun in your case—some endless symbolic meaning. For example, when Gandhi announced that he was going to the Indian Ocean and take salt out of it, salt that the British were taxing, no matter what they say or do, it is perfectly obvious that he picked salt for many reasons. It is absolutely necessary in the tropics, for one thing, but it has great symbolic value too. Now my feeling is that, in principle, what you tried to do with the gun might have had something of the same concrete and symbolic meaning, and that you did it at the right historical moment. Does that make sense or not?

JHB It makes perfect sense to me. I wish you would just be more specific, though. You used as a subtitle for the Gandhi book an expression like "the origins of militant nonviolence," and I think the concept of nonviolence as utilized by Americans with respect to blacks is quite different from what I hear you saying. It seems to me that nonviolence here has always meant acquiescence to whatever power is used against one in one's attempt to gain justice. Some moral force would come from somewhere and overcome the violent application of force. I'm not sure that is what you are saying.

EHE Not exactly. In fact, there is a similarity here which I brought out in the Gandhi book. It would be very easy to say that black people have to remain nonviolent because they'll never learn to fight anyway, and some people would say, "Well, nonviolence fits their inborn meekness and their religious orientation." Now the case is very similar with India because there you have one military caste that had done virtually all the fighting, so that the great masses of people in India never learned to use weapons at all until the British came along and drafted them into the army. Those crack Indian troops in the British Army that we heard so much about all came from warrior castes whose job on earth, decreed by heaven, was to fight. The rest of the Indians didn't know how to fight, had never had any experience with weapons, and made it a point of religious observance to do no harm to anyone. Now Gandhi (and his friends did not like him for it) would sometimes support the British demand that Indians be drafted, because he felt that Indians would have to learn to fight before they could *choose* to be nonviolent.

That's what you meant in part, isn't it? That it makes no sense
for a meek person to call himself nonviolent, because, sure, what
else can he be?

HPN   I think it would be wrong to compare other situations
to Gandhi's action. You have to leave it in context and regard it
in terms of the particular contradictions involved. Now I would
have agreed with the notion that Indians join the British Army
in order to get the training necessary to oppose the army: I can
understand that at some point it is worthwhile to play upon the
weakness of the oppressor. Gandhi did this knowing the character of the British quite well, but I think he would have acted differently here. People here who tried to act the same way he did,
I think, missed the mark and were not realistic.

JHB   Most people would say that the apostle of nonviolence
in this country with respect to blacks was Martin Luther King.
He had a clearly stated philosophy and openly expressed a debt
to Gandhi. Now I would suspect that most people, not understanding the context in which you are speaking, would expect
to see a very strong clash between your views and Huey's views
on this particular subject. And I would like to see that cleared
up, because I've always argued that there have to be certain social bases for nonviolence . . .

EHE   Look, the last thing I would wish to do is advocate
nonviolence outside of a concrete situation, particularly since it
makes exploited people all the more vulnerable. Unless one is
very careful, the whole nonviolent point of view could be used
against people rather than for them. I gave a seminar at MIT
once, and somebody brought Tom Mboya to one of the meetings. The students and I had just been discussing Gandhi, so we
asked Mboya what he thought about nonviolence. Well, he said,
you can use it with the British but you can't use it with the
Belgians. No two historical situations are ever identical in this
sense. What Mboya may have also meant was that Gandhi had
become something of a Britisher himself: he had been educated
in England, of course, and so he knew where he could count on

the British to react to nonviolence in a certain way. I guess that is really all I have to say. I just have a feeling that you are not an advocate of violence as such, you know.

HPN   No, I don't advocate violence. I advocate nonviolence. If I really had a choice, I would prefer the nonantagonistic kind of contradictions because they usually can be resolved in a peaceful way. But of course we have to deal with concrete conditions and the reality of the situation at this time is that there are many contradictions that probably can only be resolved in antagonistic ways and will probably result in violence —and this will probably be the case until man and society develop to the point where contradictions will no longer be antagonistic. So I am working for the day when antagonisms will no longer exist. And this will probably be only after people commonly own and share things.

JHB   Erik, you were saying the other day that the Panthers may understand nonviolence better than anyone else because they understand violence so well. And I was thinking about that in connection with Huey's statement that we advocate the abolition of war. We say that power grows out of the barrel of a gun, Chairman Mao's words; but we also say that the purpose of picking up the gun is to get rid of it. Now most people in this society pick up the gun for the purpose of maintaining control, and they do not understand that someone else might pick it up in order to abolish control.

HPN   Use violence in order to eliminate it.

JHB   Right. Right.

EHE   The point is that you cannot step from undisciplined violence to nonviolence. In India, Gandhi failed mostly where he could not restrain people from rioting, and you remember (I remember, at least) how he called off some of his nonviolent campaigns because rioting broke out. Now the Panthers have actually opposed violence for its own sake, isn't that right?

HPN   Nondisciplined violence, yes.

EHE   Only a very self-disciplined use of force can lead to disciplined nonviolence and the abolition of violence. And, of course, it also takes a pretty high set of moral aspirations for leaders to make people understand all of that....

KTE   O.K., the machine is on again. It's time for Oedipus and the controller.

HPN   Well, the Oedipus myth, as I understand it, is used in psychoanalysis as a symbol. The son competes for the mother's love and feels hostility toward the father because he keeps him from the mother. Now I concluded that it is not always the father per se, but the *controller* in the house. The Oedipus complex is not so much a sexual drive as a drive to eliminate the controller or take control away from the controller. As a matter of fact, that is something we have to make quite clear: eliminating the controller and assuming the place of the controller are two different things, taking on the positive and casting off the negative.

EHE   Which would then be a dialectical kind of thing, right?

HPN   Right.

EHE   You love your father and you want to become like him, but at the same time you want to get rid of him so you can replace him. So it is built into a society that you end up being more or less like your father, and represent the same to your children. Now I gather you are saying that something happens in a revolution to change that repetitive pattern, but I don't quite see . . .

HPN   That is exactly what I wanted to take note of. There's a difference between eliminating the controller and assuming control: it is possible to get rid of the controller without assuming all of his negative characteristics. One way is to not only eliminate the controller but all of his creations at the same time, although it shouldn't be done the way some people in the youth movement are doing it. It is a very immature thing to run away to communes and to plow the soil all over again—renouncing all of the technological equipment the father happened to produce because they oppose him. They are rejecting one manifestation of freedom if they do that, the freedom to choose whether to plow or not, you see

EHE   O.K., would you also include in this a certain violent faction that seems to want to destroy the whole system so that it can be reborn? And these people are willing to sacrifice all technological achievements in order . . .

HPN   To negate the whole thing. I didn't understand it at the time, but Trotsky always talked about there being no such things as particular kinds of culture, there was only continuity. So at some times a gun is quite necessary and at other times it would be proper to use other strategies, whatever will promote the victims' move toward freedom. But the Oedipus complex is as much as anything else a symbolic fight of the victim against the controller.

EHE   I wrote a paper on dissent recently for the *International Journal of Psychoanalysis*, and I took that occasion to point out that we always talk about the Oedipus complex as if only the boy's hostility was involved. But we never talk about Laius, the father of Oedipus, and ask what "complex" made him so ready to believe the oracle that his little boy was going to kill him someday. He believed it so strongly that he put the baby Oedipus out, exiled him. We won't understand the repetitiveness of this pattern unless we realize the importance of the fact that the king believed in the son's potential threat instead of trusting his own ability to bring up the little boy in such a way that the oracle would have been disproven. That would not make a myth, I know, but it might make history. Why do we not point to the ways in which every establishment and every established organization, out of a fear that the young will overcome them, limit the identities of the young and permit them access to adulthood only by way of confirmations, communions, inductions, and so on—every one of which limits the young to a particular identity and threatens transgressors? And, of course, war comes in here in the sense that every pseudospecies would put their young into particular uniforms and try to impress them by way of historical mythology that the highest affirmation of life would be a heroic death for the system. If you die well, you're going to be immortal—and all the more so if you first kill many representatives of the other pseudospecies *ad majoram gloriam* of your own pseudospecies.

KTE   Who are also young.

EHE   Who are also young. They kill each other off, then, and at the end the two systems make peace with each other, having killed enough of the best fighters in each other's younger generation to have avoided a certain potential for rebellion in their own country.

KTE   Boy. That's quite a thought.

HPN   Yes, it is.

EHE   There is something to that, don't you think? But nowadays the young of countries that a very short time ago were ready to do this to each other periodically, like the Germans and the French, are suddenly beginning to recognize that they are in many ways closer to each other than they are to their respective parents.

HPN   That is because they are becoming one community. That is what intercommunalism is all about.

KTE   The people to whom this is becoming most obvious —in this country, at least—are the young who realize that it is always other young people they go to war with and blacks who realize that is it usually exploited people they go to war with.

HPN   That's right.

EHE   There is another matter that we may not want to try to get at today, but which we should mention as a background for the future. Once the young have agreed on standing up against a system that imposes a form of filicide on the young of the world, there may well follow a tendency toward fratricide, which is probably part of all revolutions. You mentioned Trotsky: remember how—in spite of Lenin, who was probably the most balanced of all those men—how in the end Stalin made of himself (again) the one father, the traditional "little father," heir to the Russian tradition with all its capacity for tyranny? Now maybe the world is closer today to a revolutionary fraternity and sorority; but what are people going to do to keep one another from assuming the roles of older brothers and sisters? The questions always is: When you gain a new measure of freedom, who can claim the right to sanction it? The fact that man has such a long childhood may be the evolutionary origin of his tendency to always search for an older figure who will sanction whatever license he takes. Even if rebels first kill the father and then kill each other, there always comes the question —who is going to be that charismatic older brother who sanctions the license you took and confirms your right to have taken it? And then some of the brothers will fight each other for the role of the oldest. The result, as we can see even in some of the abortive revolutionary developments of today, can be paralysis, and then depression, lethargy, and a re-emergence of the old moralisms in revolutionary disguise; for man cannot destroy the old without some kind of sanction. I have a feeling that revolutions have been very costly for this reason—costly in a way that man today, with the means of mechanical destruction available to him, simply cannot afford. Let's just take Stalin as a historical example— no matter who in that revolutionary development you are most for. My God, what if he had had an atomic arsenal at his disposal? What might have happened then?

HPN   Well, what did happen? This country had the weapons, and look: Nagasaki, Hiroshima.

EHE   O.K. You've got me there. That's what we should talk about tomorrow—Hiroshima, the moon, and America. I would like to try out some notes on you.

HPN   You mentioned that revolutions are costly, and I just wanted to say that they are not themselves costly and negative: it's the kind of friction, the kind of obstacles that are in the way of revolution that keep the change at the antagonistic level, you see. But the process of revolution, the process of change, the new struggling against the old to produce some synthesis, does not necessarily have to be a destructive process.

EHE   Well, I hope you are right.

Oakland, California, April 1, 1971

KTE   Could I start off by asking a question? One of the common grounds between Newton's ideology, Erikson's psychology, and the various notions that Herman and I bring in from the sociological outfield—he can play left field and I will play center—is the realization that a person's perception of reality is more or less shaped by the experiences he has had and by the position he occupies in the world. That's good dialectical materialism, good psychoanalysis, and good sociology all at once, right? Now we have made a lot of the fact that one of our principals is a seventy-year-old white man, an immigrant to this country, while the other is a thirty-year-old black man who comes out of a very different set of circumstances. To be true to the logic of our various methods, then, we would have to say that these circumstances are the lens—if that is the word— through which we look at reality. I would like to hear each of you talk about those circumstances for a while.

HPN   I think it is easy for any person who accepts the ideology of dialectical materialism to share the methods and subject matters of all other disciplines, because all scientists are concerned one way or another with dialectics if they practice a true science. That's why I think that, despite age differences, the discipline of psychology and the approach of dialectical materialism would necessarily share many things in common— beginning with the developmental process and the recognition of the internal contradictions in all things. That is why it is not surprising to me, although it may be surprising to other people, that we could come to agreement on some things and at least discuss a number of things that are of interest to both of us.

KTE   Right. That's what my question is all about. There is a destination out there in the middle distance, let's say. Huey reasons his way to that destination by dialetics and Pop reasons his way there by a more psychoanalytic kind of logic. We have talked a lot about how similar the destinations seem to be, but we have not said much about the different paths you took to get there—or about the different travelers, for that matter. See what I mean? Maybe the Harvard professor will say a word about the Yale professor's question.

EHE   Well, you are right. There are a number of things I didn't spell out when I talked about myself as an immigrant. During a lifetime like mine, one can actually witness the kinds of transformation which you, Huey, describe—contradictions meeting each other and change taking place. Now my experience is that even some of the most trite and commonplace characterizations of the American Dream hold psychologically and have to be taken care of in any American's self-appraisal. When one comes from Europe, America impresses one as the first self-made nation, creating itself out of immigrants who came from all the different pseudospecies of the world and converged here. They had to create a new nation and to become nationals of a new kind. And that nation became a new kind of industrial empire, certainly different from the British one. The British Empire created a superidentity too—we don't have to go into that—but at least there always was an England—an ancient geographical core, a self-contained island . . .

HPN   One empire is based upon tradition, the other empire is based upon technocracy—and that's a new kind of nation in itself.

EHE   But technocracy was not the original idea. The coming together of technocracy with a self-made nation was—in

some ways, at least—almost a historical coincidence, even
though a new nation with a whole wide continent to expand in
had what it needed as the base of a new technocratic empire.
Historically, then, the "self-made" idea and the technocratic vision fused into an idealized image of a man who almost literally made himself, created himself, manufactured himself, invented himself. This is important to point out because what we
call the American empire is really a universal technocracy with
America in the role not only of central power but also of central
value-giver. And the main value we export is that of the self-
made man. In Germany and Japan, for instance, people who belong to the establishment have to some extent accepted that
basic value, and even in India you can see it reflected very
sharply in the new managerial class. Compared to others, they
look American, talk American, live like Americans in apartment
houses, and are beginning to develop a new family structure
and a new set of values to go along with it. Now I would argue
that the self-made man is a new kind of pseudospecies—a type
of person who by temperament and opportunity can make of
himself pretty much what he wants to and who considers other
pseudospecies to be people who cannot do all of that for reasons
of race or class or type or weakness or something else. Of course,
the Indians (American, this time) who happened to be situated
here and the blacks whose immigration was not exactly self-
chosen were very useful to the image of a pseudospecies that
likes to think they came here of their own free will—or by God's
choice.

    HPN   I would like to question the whole concept of the
self-made man. The people who settled America were not self-
made, but were the product of specific social and historical circumstances. The people who came to America were outcasts,
they were victims; and the state they established was quite different from the traditional kind of empire. Now as we were
saying a while ago, we can see that people sometimes—probably most of the time—arrive at a certain level of power without

this power being shared in a universal sense. They become the new status quo and they attempt to hold back the process again. And once they try to stop the process of change they take on the form of the father, of the controller. Only now, with a new kind of technocracy at their disposal—transportation, mass media, and so on—their influence is so great that they reach everyone in the whole world. Now this is dialectical in itself, because as their control becomes more severe and more encompassing, the more enemies they make. And this is why I say that the whole world has become one community in the hands of the old victim, who is now the new lord, you see. This is reactionary intercommunalism. The downfall of this new self-made man, then, is going to be that people will rebel against him because of his insistence that he has all of the answers. This is why reactionary intercommunalism, while it causes its own destruction, also lays the foundation for its own transformation; because without modern communication and all the rest of it, how would the youth of the world develop a common identity? A sense of themselves as oppressed?

EHE   Well, you and I will always have a certain problem with words, probably. When I speak of the self-made man, of course, I am not saying that he *was* self-made or that he came to America for that purpose: I am talking about the *image* he had of himself and the way that image fed into his ideal identity. So I am talking about myth rather than history, about the way men mythologize the facts of history as they develop newer and wider identities. At any rate, what I meant to emphasize is that for the immigrants and their children the image of the self-made man and the vision of technological proficiency went together— and that even today that American ideal is spreading all over the world in one form or another, contributing to what you call reactionary intercommunalism despite our libertarian history. This ideal serves to maintain and to protect the ruthless kind of business which leaves out those who do not help themselves— and here you can underline either "help *themselves*" or "*help* themselves (to it)," as you choose. I guess all I am saying is that in one lifetime or even one adulthood (FDR was president when I came) the idea of the country liberating others from bondage has become reversed—so that the country is now experienced by some of its own youth as a new empire, a ruthless technocracy, led (or misled) by a thoughtless and greedy power elite. It certainly would never have occurred to me at the time of my immigration as a refugee from European fascism to suspect any fascist potential in the American system. When you are welcomed as an immigrant, it is hard to look around and ask whom from abroad they are not letting in—and whom at home they are keeping down to a level below that of any newcomer. And perhaps this would be a good time for me to add that people like myself, who kept a close and personal eye on the emergence of Nazism in Germany, will never be able to use the word "fascism" as casually as it is sometimes used in radical circles today.

JHB   Well, let me pursue this matter of fascist potential, Erik, from the more subjective perspective you were talking about. Americans felt that they had come here of their own free will and saw themselves as self-made men—I am talking about self-perceptions rather than objective conditions here—and this brought them to the conviction that they were somehow destined to develop a new identity at the expense of blacks and of Indians. Now that's where the fascist potential is, Erik: our society is based upon the principle that some people are empowered to deny other people their rights as human beings. . . .

KTE   Let me try something out here. When people use the term "exploitation," they are usually thinking in economic terms: there is a limited supply of money in society, so people exploit one another to get as large a share of that scarce resource as they can. But there are other resources considered to be scarce in society even though the supply is theoretically unlimited—dignity, for example, or prestige. Now the fact is that the self-made man, however he got his wealth, earned his self-esteem, his proud sense of self, by depreciating the dignity of other people. He measured his worth as a human being not just by his holdings but by his social distance from other people whom he needed to see as less worthy—and who did the work he saw as demeaning. All of this obvious, I suppose, in the case of blacks. But it was also true of women. You can bet that for every self-made, self-reliant spirit who celebrated his manhood by roaring up and down the frontier there was a woman somewhere in a kind of bondage, dependent upon the circumstances in which she found herself to almost exactly the same degree that he was *in*dependent of them. They say it takes several other soldiers to support one front-line troop; well, I imagine that it takes several other persons to support one self-made man, too, because he has to draw off the dignity and freedom of so many other people to enhance his own. And the irony is that the support troops usually accept his definition of the situation: they, too, believe that there is not enough dignity to go around, that the only way for somebody to increase his own stature is to diminish somebody else's. Incidentally (or maybe it's not so incidental at that) one of the ways in which the youth movement has broken with the American tradition is that the kids seem to think there is enough dignity and love and honor for everyone. It is positively un-American.

EHE   One of you asked me yesterday how I would put into my terms the role of a Black Panther at this time in history and in this place. Well, I think I explained that every new pseudo-species, as it stakes out its territory and its methods and its lifestyle, must project its implicit negative identity on some other kind of man—either an enemy beyond the borders or a slave of some kind within them. And it is obvious in America that the blacks are the largest and, in the historical sense, the most "opposite" group in this self-made business, not only because they didn't come over here of their own free will but also because their color marked them as a most recognizable "other" species. Now the black man in this country, of course, also absorbed some of the values of the self-made man, and his "suffering" of an inferior position—both in the sense of suffering acutely and of an unconscious acceptance of it, a kind of overadaption—was intensified by the discrepancy between the American values he was aware of and the limited opportunities given to him in sharing them. So for every group to be liberated, it is essential to realize sooner or later that they themselves absorbed the dominant values that enslaved them and, in fact, based their identities on them. This is where the psychology of the unconscious enters, although it is obvious that the to-be-liberated should take a close look at psychological methods to make sure that they are not accepting what was invented to fortify the status quo. But now, the second item that I was after is the dialectic of the self-appraisal of the dominant pseudospecies when it overreaches itself and loses its own identity exactly out of overdoing that original identity. If that original identity was an overcoming of old unfreedoms by an emphasis on the self-made man's individualism, it does not prevent him, before he knows it, from becoming the most stereotyped type of person in the world. You see what I mean? In other words, you can go on talking about the rights of the individual in all public announcements and yet be ready to be told what types and what styles to choose as a "consumer" of values—thereby denying to your children the capacity to be an individual. So we now have schools all over the nation that preach individualism and encourage the individualist stance, but cannot permit any true freedom of learning. You can see this on many levels. So what is happening at the moment is that the American way of life, wherever the American empire goes, fosters the same efficient personality types who are "nobody's fools"—that is, the sort of people one finds in the police, in the army, or among the ranks of technocrats and bureaucrats who have the mandate of protecting the system against messy "outsiders," here and abroad. The typical "insider" neither knows how much stereotypy he accepts in himself to bolster his own sense of playing a "free" role shared with others, nor how much inhuman method he fosters in those middlemen whom he has put in uniforms and uniformed roles and charged with protecting his "privacy" against any first-hand knowledge of those his system enslaves. This is what makes it possible that, for example, American airmen who consider themselves nice guys, individualists, and technically proficient all at once, can do what they do to an "other" people down in those "jungles" in Vietnam today. And yet, a change must come from within this country and it makes sense that some of it must come from you blacks. Obviously, something is crumbling in the whole American system, a change in America's sense of itself; they call it "consciousness" at Yale. But it needs militant minorities, and by sheer impact you are probably the most effective on the domestic scene for shaking up the old self-images—and that is why I pointed to the "black with a gun" imagery.

EHE Once the American experience was underway, it created quantitative extremes which meant that gradually the quality was lost. That quantitative overreach can be physical expansion to the size of an empire, or it can be the overproduction of goods, or it can be a readiness for overkill, or it can be a personal sense of unlimited possibilities. One can make a long list. A new model is needed, and that means a new and wider and more inclusive identity. Your idea of community or communalism, then—again by the logic of dialectics—should include all of those who have been excluded from that overreaching vision and who therefore have preserved certain qualities which success alone has not been able to preserve. That is what I meant the other day when I said that you are really talking about the great unbroken quality of black life— by which I do not mean "stick to your music."

JHB The point I have been trying to make is that the changes we are talking about require a new character definition, new definitions of self—but that is only going to come about as a result of hard, hard struggle. And those youth who are seeking a new identity must divest themselves of the old identity based on quantity and more quantity. I just don't see that as a very likely prospect.

EHE   I know. But to me, identity has to do with terrific power struggles as well as with terrific delusions. It is a matter of life and death, and not just a conscious choice of what kind of nice identity one would like to have. To me, identity means what the best in you lives by, the loss of which would make you less human. Let me just add one thing. All the way from Germany to Japan, the youth of the world—the more thoughtful and militant young people, at any rate—have felt in the center of what you call the inner contradictions in the whole expansion. The youth of many countries suddenly saw that this expansion did not give them a basis for identity, and in that sense the identity based on technological expansion had already within it the seed of what you always call the "opposite." Exactly those parents who became the most successful and most technocratically dominant people suddenly began to look like robots to their children. And this happened in family after family. Now the whole theory of identity itself may be too closely related to a past era, an era of wanting to *be* somebody or to be *somebody*. But when you teach at Harvard today and you see the children of all those successful people, it is striking how little it means to them—or so they pretend—what their parents are. Now this is not just a fad, a passing mood: the fact is, I think, that they do not get from their parents' way of life the necessary identity strengths. So something is happening across the nation—the world, for that matter—and maybe the Panthers have been in a key spot here in developing a strong and clear fraternal image.

KTE   I sense a pause. Could I steer you back to the question of how and where one's ideas originate?

EHE   Oh, that. Well, I gave a paper the other day for a meeting of scientists in Europe, each of whom were being asked why *they*, of all people, were the first to think of a particular word or concept or theory which afterward seemed so self-evident to everybody. And I was asked: Why were you the first to write about "identity crisis" in a systematic way? Now when I first used the notion, I had no idea what impact it would have, and I tried to describe in that paper—I'll send you a copy—how within a few years it had spread to other countries. Now I related a number of details about my background in that paper, and I probably shouldn't repeat them here, but I might mention a couple of things. I never knew my own father, for one thing, and I belonged to a mixed racial and religious background. But most of all, I came to this country at the time when *it* entered into something of an identity crisis, just because it had tried to make out of the descendants of so many different pseudospecies one new one. So the American identity was in some ways a manufactured one, a self-invented one, and . . .

HPN   And I would say that it is a necessarily oppressive one.

EHE   Well, all right, but so is every other identity that comes from the same source. Let me try to say it in one sentence, and then I will be through. As long as the core of any collective identity is a pseudospecies idea, it is going to be oppressive. As long as the Britishers felt chosen by God to colonize all those African and Asian countries, they were bound to be oppressive—although they did create a new conscience at the same time. America, too, for a long time could ignore the fact that it was bound to be oppressive in order to spread new ideas along with new methods of production.

HPN   But when we create a spirit of oneness, it won't be oppressive.

EHE   That is, I think, what Marx meant way back when he spoke of an overcoming of history itself, an idea probably related to that of the withering away of the state.

HPN   I think that you understand reactionary and revolutionary intercommunalism very well. You put it in somewhat different words, but I can agree with almost everything you say. Just before I went to Yale, I told the class at our Inter-communal Institute that I did not know how I was going to fare there because your writings had taken the wind out of my argument. I had thought at first that I would just be dealing with another psychoanalyst, but after I read some of your things I found it difficult to treat you as an adversary. But at the same time, I felt that I could not just go there and agree with you because of my own situation in the Party. So you see the dilemma I was in. And I felt a little robbed, too, because I had worked very hard to put my ideas together, and here someone else had already laid a number of them out. That is somewhat frustrating, you know.

KTE   This may be the time for me to pursue my favorite question again, the one with which we began this morning. The way Huey hacked through the forest to arrive at the idea of communalism is very different from the way Pop hacked through the forest to arrive at the idea of identity, even if the two products look a lot alike. Now Pop said a word or two about the circumstances that could help explain why he was the person to write about identity and the identity crisis. So, Huey, why do you suppose you were the person to come up with the idea of intercommunalism? Would it be fair to ask you how you made your way through that forest?

HPN   Personally, I am not sure I know.

EHE   Why do you think you invented intercommunalism?

HPN   Well, I didn't invent it. I discovered it, focused upon it.

EHE   O.K. I didn't invent identity crisis either—although, come to think of it, some of my friends seemed to think that I *did* invent it, and out of my own conflicts too. I had to try to show them that if this were so, at least my own conflicts were in the right place at the right time, historically speaking.

HPN   A scientist, if he is also an activist, will necessarily go about changing things in a different way than a laborer, let's say, or someone else who does not have any particular discipline, you see. So I went into activism with a scientific method, and . . .

EHE   But why? That's the point. There must have been something in your background, in your choice of parents, in the place where you grew up, which made you that independent. If you consider only how many of your brothers just accepted what they were taught, or accepted being excluded from what was being taught, while you always insisted on your right to study and your right to teach. There's always a personal quality to a man which cannot be reduced to explanations. That's obvious. But you must have some idea what . . .

HPN   Well, I don't know how important it is. I seldom discuss my own personal life except as it relates to the movement.

EHE   I seldom do either. In fact, I only talk about myself in relation to the identity concept, as you will see when you read that paper. I think one has the right—maybe even the duty—to restrict oneself to that: otherwise everything becomes a kind of self-indulgence.

HPN   I think one of the things that would naturally make me somewhat freer to take an objective approach to situations rather than just follow what has been traditional is the fact that I am the seventh sibling in my family. I am the youngest and my family is very tightly knit; my father and mother have been married almost fifty years now, I guess. I was protected, you know, taken care of; and in a situation like that one is usually a little rebellious. In order to assert myself, I would act somewhat aggressive.

EHE   How many brothers and how many sisters?

HPN   Three brothers and three sisters. And, as I say, I was the youngest. It is almost a book in itself to tell you how I was torn between my brothers and my sisters. I took on the characteristics of all of them, in a way, and by doing that I was bound to be transformed, you see, because how could I identify with all of them and at the same time maintain the thing that was characteristic of the family? I could see, let's say, identifying with my father or my mother and coming out with the kind of personality that is either just the opposite or very much the same as either of them. But I developed a relationship with all of them and appreciated all of their personalities—and that made me different from them. It made me a stranger in a way.

EHE   But don't you think that as the youngest you were also very important to all of them and that they made you feel important? I would assume that this was so, in spite of the fact that the youngest always feels oppressed because the others are so big.

HPN   Well, I felt loved by everyone in the family. Not necessarily important, but loved.

EHE   Was it clear from the outset—obviously it became clear later—that you were going to be the last child also? How old was your mother when you were born?

HPN   Well, she was fourteen when she was married. She must have been around twenty-nine when I was born. Maybe thirty or thirty-two.

EHE   And how about that move west to Oakland? Oakland seems important to me somehow, but I can't figure out why.

HPN   You know, I didn't leave Oakland until after I got out of prison except for two trips to Los Angeles. I didn't leave for the whole twenty-five years. I came here when I was one or two years old.

EHE   Do you think Oakland has something to do with all of this? Oakland and the West?

HPN   As a social scientist, I would say that wherever we are has a definite influence on us, and what we have to do is find out the difference between one area and another.

EHE   Well, you probably know what I am driving at. I have been impressed, as I said more than once, that there seems to be a strong western influence in the Black Panther image.

JHB   I was just thinking about the time the idea of inter-communalism came into the picture. I remember coming over to your place, Huey, the day that you started talking about intercommunalism, and I can say very honestly that I have rarely seen you as excited as you were then. You told us that it was a vision. But if you look at it in terms of its materialistic basis, it was a vision which came as the result of trying to put together a lot of different concepts in some comprehensive way. You were handling and juggling a lot of them then.

HPN   That's right. I was not satisfied with a statement that I was writing to the Vietnamese because there was a contradiction in it. Let me share this with you. I was telling the Vietnamese that the Party supported their nationalism, their revolutionary nationalism, even though we were not nationalists. We were internationalists and could not be nationalists: no Americans could afford to be nationalists because we are all guilty on one level or another of being the exploiter or accepting the bribe of the exploiter if we are not at war with him. So I said that I disclaim nationalism because it is a thing of the past but that I would support their nationalism nonetheless. I disclaimed all of the black nationalists in that statement—and, of course, that brought about a bad relationship between our Party and other black organizations because all of them, even the bourgeois ones, are somewhat nationalistic in tone and in goal. Now if we disclaim nationalism for ourselves and yet support nationalism for those other people, then it seems as though we are belittling them, being traitors to them. So I sent the statement to them, but I was very dissatisfied and unhappy for about a month. I kept tossing this around in my mind and suppressing it in a way. Then I woke up one morning with this concept of intercommunalism, and it was like a vision: it didn't seem as coldly calculated as when you work out a mathematical problem, which is how I usually handle things intellectually. I just woke up that morning and I had solved the contradiction in my sleep. And I was excited to get it out. I have had the experience in the past of having a dream or vision and then forgetting the damn thing because I didn't get it down. I was anxious to get all of this down in writing so that I could refer to it. And that is the history of that concept.

EHE   Now you are a revolutionary and I obviously am not. But . . .

HPN   Some people say I'm not either.

EHE   But, as you say, several of our ideas are complementary in the sense that even though one can only go so far in bringing them together, they still relate closely to one another. Let me illustrate what I mean by relating what you have been saying to some concerns of mine about children and education. It is terribly important for communalism that children should live in a true community in order to develop a sense of identity that is communally based, as it were. Identity is both an individual and a communal concept because you cannot have a sense of identity—or better, you cannot grow a sense of identity step for step through the life stages—without anchoring it somewhere in a group setting. Children, obviously, have only a fragmentary capacity to understand the world. At first, the child's mother *is* the world, and then he learns to interact with a limited number of people at given times.

HPN   At first, only with himself.

EHE   But even there, way back at the beginning, everything depends upon the way he is handled, the way he is nursed, all of which already expressed a community's style—so in that sense, he is never alone. Even the way the mother gives him the breast already expresses a communal style, because in different communities people do such things differently—what they *say* when they do it, how *long* they do it, the *way* they do it, and so on. There the child has already begun to be a member of the community. So much depends upon the parents' relationship to the rest of the community, too, for example whether the community gives them a peaceful and purposeful sense of administering to small children. I would say, then, that in intercommunalism groups would have to be interrelated sufficiently to assure children a sense of identity in a wider world, which could only happen if the rest of the world developed a common style of bringing up the children.

HPN Yes, this is what would be necessary to stop the antagonistic kind of contradiction on the group or tribal or national level. But the only point I want to emphasize now—and I know you understand it—is that the process is usually very bloody because the identity that is forced on people is often based on hostility. . . . When I was young and working in the Black Muslims and other organizations, we were required to hate all white people. I would find myself being courteous to whites, and they would call me to check on it. Now I could understand intellectually and academically that I had the right to treat whites as roughly as I wanted, because they had the upper hand; but I would just find myself reacting differently. One time I saw a girl at one of our functions who was extremely light skinned with Caucasian features, and she kept trying to convince them that she was black. They wouldn't hear her. They abused her and said she was really disturbed, you know, and she kept telling them that she was from Louisiana and wasn't white. It really hurt me. The tone was one of hostility the moment she walked in the door. Maybe I can relate that back to my family, I don't know; but within my family the cue was never color because there is a big difference of color in it. I remember that when I was a baby—I was just on the sideline then—my brother and sister would call one of my sisters "Red" when they got angry with her, and she would break down in tears. At the same time, some of the others would call the darkest one in the family a black bitch, you see, and then she would be broken up. My father had very straight hair and others had very curly hair, like my own. So I never thought that color was the way to tell people apart. I knew the difference between white people and black people, of course, but the cue was always the way white people treated us, not the color itself. Do you see what I mean? Maybe that was one of my problems in the early stages of the movement. Even now I would say that intercommunalism has something to do with this.

JHB   What you are saying is that you did not sense hostility from some whites and therefore you did not respond to them with hostility.

HPN   No, I'm saying that even if I expected and received a hostile kind of response from whites in most situations, my feeling would be related to something other than the fact that they happened to be very light skinned, you see. So when a girl came in who looked white to me, I was willing to accept her as a black the minute she said she wasn't white. I didn't care how light skinned she was. Herman, do you remember the hang-ups people like Malcolm X and Garvey had about skin color? Well, I can appreciate their concern about it, but this never affected me, you see what I mean? Because of the nature of oppression and the way the world is today, people identify each other by color. The Muslims personify the whole thing by saying that "white is evil," you see, and this is the kind of thing that is hard for me to accept. . . . What I'm saying is that I need something else than color to judge people. For example, I often open doors for people without even noticing that they are white or giving it a thought; but I can be very, very hostile toward someone if he gives any indication whatever of feeling superior. Now most white people have a kind of opposition to me just because I am black, you see, so they have their cue but I do not have mine.

EHE   May I ask one question? You spoke of your particular place in the family. Did your family have a particular place in the community?

HPN   Yes, we were victims. My father is an uneducated man, no formal education, although he is a very wise man. We were from a farming community and before I was born my father was a sharecropper. He married very early: my mother was fourteen and he was eighteen. Then he moved here to

Oakland with seven children right after I was born and worked in the shipyards. My father always had at least three jobs to support the family, and that's another part of my own rebellion: I don't have a family and I probably never will.

EHE   Was your father somewhat different from the rest of the community? Did you perceive him as typical or unique?

HPN   Well, one of the problems my father had with people was that he was very light skinned with straight hair, and they could say that he was different from other blacks. He would take exception to that, though, and say that he was no different and would rather be treated like every other member of his group. He would not accept any favors. He told us later that foremen on jobs would say, "You don't want to do this work, the other guys can do it; you can be truck driver." But he would say, "No. I'd rather not be a truck driver; I'll sweep the streets." So people attempted to treat him differently, but he would not accept it.

EHE   Well, then, he was different in not letting them *make* him different.

HPN   Of course.

EHE   So in many ways you came from a more stable family than most blacks do.

HPN   My father went up to about eighth grade or so. He's not professional, although he has many skills. He lays brick, he's a cement mason, and he's a carpenter; but he does not have any credentials, so he would have to do all of this for a handyman's price. As I said, he would work three jobs to take care of seven children. He was a stable figure and we always depended upon him. My mother has never worked—she was always in the house having children or taking care of them—so he would have to do everything: pay all the bills, do three jobs, everything. Now I may be searching again for explanations, but one of the reasons I do not have a family or ever hope to have one other than the Party is that I have always identified with the sufferings of my father. I felt that he was captured. All he would do is work, and then he would send me around Oakland to pay all of the bills until the money was gone. This would happen every two weeks, and I decided that I would never be a slave like that. He was a slave, you see. He did it because he loved us, and we in turn loved him; but at the same time I rebelled against it. . . .

KTE   So the Party will be your family?

HPN   The Party requires a good deal of sacrifice, but in order to sacrifice you need love. You know, Herbert Hendin has pointed out in a recent book that black suicide is different from white suicide: 80 percent of all black suicides occur, he says, because of the lack or loss of a lover—although I would just want to say lack or loss of love in general. Whites commit suicide because they suffer the loss of prestige or position or economic security, but blacks commit suicide for lack of love because this is all we have. If love is gone, there is no reason to go on—and this is how I feel about the Party. I am willing to make any sacrifice, not because of a suicidal tendency on my part, as some psychologists and sociologists have concluded, but because the sacrifice is compensated through the fraternity. But then the question arises at this stage of the game: what happens after the fraternity is broken, you see? Where's the reinforcement going to come from?

EHE   Well, that brings us back to the whole question of the fraternal and fratricidal relations of revolutionaries.

HPN   Is that a necessary part of development though?

EHE   The matter of brothers and sisters forming a community is a theme in all development, I suppose, but it seems to become an acute problem of leadership in revolutions. I watched you on television the other day when your old friend [Eldridge Cleaver] broke with you, and I couldn't help thinking (you may not want to discuss this here at all): What do brothers do to each other once it becomes a matter of struggling for power among equals?

HPN   The struggle for power among the brothers may be

a natural outgrowth of eliminating the father, but it will probably hurt more than the struggle between the son and the father because divorce is sharper. It is more devastating. But I don't know if I agree with you that this is a natural kind of outgrowth. I just don't know.

EHE I didn't mean that. What I meant is that different historical situations bring out different aspects of man's learned patterns. And if this is so, then maybe it would be better to understand those patterns in order to control them better. There can be such a waste of human resources when the simplest emotions are misunderstood.

HPN I think it would be fair to state that there is no real difference between familyhood and tribalism and no real difference between tribalism and nationhood. They all depend upon a sense of identity that is exclusive, you see—and this is even true of what they call internationalism.

JHB When you say there is no difference, do you mean there is no difference in principle or in kind between, say, tribalism and nationhood?

HPN There is only a quantitative difference between familyhood and tribalism and between tribalism and nationhood, not a qualitative difference.

JHB But relationships between people in a family setting and a tribal setting are much more primary, whereas in a national setting they are more likely to be secondary.

HPN I agree. It's impossible to have a face-to-face relationship between one hundred or two hundred million people. But it's still a matter of degree. At first, people say: "I will defend my family and serve my family because we share a common history, a common value system, a common ethnic background, and a common religion." Then as society grows a number of families come together in a close relationship, and say: "We have the same past, the same values—we are a tribe."

Then the tribes compete with one another for territory until they merge into nations, and it's the same thing all over again on a different scale: "I will defend my nation because we share a common background, common principles and values," and so on. I would say that the concept of the nation is strictly related to the concept of the family, and that there is only a quantitative difference between the two.

JHB   So what is the next step?

HPN   Well, in order for man to survive there has to be some universal identity that extends beyond family, tribe, or nation—an identity that is essentially human and does not depend upon people thinking that others are something less than they are.

EHE   The trouble with that comparison is that the family is essentially meant for bringing up children, while nations . . .

HPN   You are saying that the family is the traditional method for bringing up children. I would say that the family has always been a traditional way of keeping people children.

KTE   Huey, when we were talking about the Oedipus complex a little while back, you said something about science and religion that intrigued me.

HPN   Science constantly challenges the whole idea of the supernatural and God is, you know, the symbol of the father. Now once you reach a maturity in consciousness, then you assume the role of God yourself. Whenever science discovers something new, all of a sudden the church starts to say that it is now an earthly thing: it is not related to God anymore, but God still exists. So when does God stop existing? He stops existing as soon as you bite the fruit of knowledge and can assume control yourself. But you haven't really destroyed God; you have become God. You have become the controller yourself. The point is that a *will to power* is the primary drive of man, not the sexual drive. It is an attempt to reverse the dominance in nature—to become the controller, to become the father, to become God. As long as other people control us, we remain children. As Erik pointed out, that is why Marx said that there can be no real adults in a capitalist society.

EHE On the subject of controllers and fathers: what is happening right now to the leaders of the revolution in a wider sense? What form do you expect leadership to take in the future?

HPN I think in the future people will realize more and more that they are responsible for creating leadership just as they are responsible for creating God. Groups create leaders just as they create other things, but they usually lose their awareness that this is so and begin to feel that the leaders are external to them, somebody to whom they must submit. So I would think that in the immediate future leadership will take more the form of the "chairmanship"—and in the distant future, although I can't really visualize it yet, leadership will become a coordinated effort among people and maybe even titles or statuses will no longer be necessary.

EHE You know, we seem to be talking around things again. I don't quite understand your concept of God, for one thing. Obviously, to say that somebody or something is the father of all people is to say that all people are brothers: the common father guarantees the brotherhood. So one question we should keep in mind is whether brotherhood can survive the loss of fatherhood. In your Party, you use terms like "brother" and "sister," but you really don't have much in the way of father images, do you? The leaders of the Party look and sound more like older brothers in your publications. Of course Ho Chi Minh comes in every once in a while . . .

HPN But they call him *Uncle* Ho.

EHE See? They call him Uncle, the father's brother. Now how about Mao, is he a father image? He seems so much more like a grandfather—who, in fact, is trying to weaken any new consolidation of father images in the hierarchy. Is that right?

HPN Yes.

KTE The next question has to be: Huey, how does a

leader like you manage to avoid becoming a "father" when you get older? How do you avoid that kind of imagery in a movement that sooner or later is going to embrace two or maybe even three generations?

HPN Who knows? Everything is in a state of transformation, nothing is stable, and the Party, too, will be transformed.

KTE But the kind of imagery the Party uses is going to have to change to take your old age into account.

EHE There is something very simple to be said here which is that both a father and a god are irreversible. You cannot say that somebody is an ex-father—either he was a father or he wasn't—and nobody can be an ex-god. But then there are other forms of leadership, aren't there, and being a teacher is one of them. I am impressed how much Mao played the role later on of the teacher, the leader who would formulate things like the sages of old.

JHB Well, Huey, I would say that you are more of a teacher than a leader or a father figure—a teacher in the sense that your approach is to provide people with processes by which they can arrive at answers rather than give them the answers themselves. That is what you are doing when you talk about states of change, internal contradictions, processes of development, transformations, and so on.

EHE Can I ask one last question? Huey, what do you think of the two-party system?

HPN Well, if there were a two-party system, maybe I would think well of it.

EHE O.K. I was just thinking about constitutional rights, existing constitutional rights. Would you expect intercommunalism to change the political structures of the various countries?

HPN Yes, I would. I believe that contradictions will be around for quite some time yet. I won't say "forever," because that's an absolute, but I cannot stretch my imagination far enough to see a time when contradictions will no longer exist.

What I do look forward to is the time when contradictions will be nonantagonistic, and I don't think that will occur until we resolve the question of property—of the property class and the class that owns no property, of the haves and the have-nots, of the contradictions based on economic interests. I feel that to resolve those contradictions it will be necessary to have a redistribution of wealth. Revolutionary intercommunalism will exist when power is distributed on an intercommunal level and each community of the world has control of its own institutions.

KTE I guess that's it. Let's close by agreeing that we've all earned a drink.